Endorsements for *We Are The Branches*

Rarely will you find such a focused, vulnerable, and bold collection of poems. If you're already a Christian, prepare to be stretched. If you don't consider yourself "saved," get ready to be Rocked! Judi Doxey is the real-deal believer and one who is not afraid to show her guts and scars. Like the Psalms of David, these concise poems will challenge, convict, and comfort you. A comprehensive collection by an experienced and mature Christian woman that deserves much attention—and celebration.

Geoff Pope, English Instructor, Northwest University, Kirkland, Washington; Editor, www.book-editing.com

Judi Doxey has an incredible soul that shows through in her poetry and art. Her words are refreshingly transparent as she honestly records her life experience in a manner that is both uplifting and challenging. I think that both youth and adults will be encouraged to grow spiritually and pursue an honest relationship with the Lord through her writings. Grab this book, a cup of good coffee, and find a quiet place to enjoy them both.

Jimmy Higgins, Youth Pastor, Grace Community Church, Ramona, California

Initially, Judi's book, *We Are The Branches*, explodes with challenge, not only the challenges she, herself, encountered to come to faith but the challenge she so ably sets before those who scoff at or flee from faith. Beyond this, Judi uses her poetry, story, and song to touch our hearts so that we not only apprehend those around us but God as well.

Andrew R. Graham, Pastor, Warner Springs Community Church, Warner Springs, California

WE ARE THE BRANCHES

Poems, Prayers, and Promises

John 15:5—"I am the vine; you are the branches.
If any man remains in Me and I in him, he will bear
much fruit; apart from Me you can do nothing."

WE ARE THE BRANCHES

Poems, Prayers, and Promises

Judith Doxey

Cover and Illustrations by Judith Doxey
Back Cover Photo by Gia Taber

We Are The Branches
Poems, Prayers, and Promises
by Judith Doxey

Printed in the United States of America

ISBN 978-1-60647-460-0

TXu 1-572-519

Also by the author:

No Turning Back

www.xulonpress.com

…And He that sat upon
the throne said, "Behold, I make
all things new." And He said
unto me, "Write: For these
words are true and faithful."

Revelation 21:5

I believe that the scriptures have but one literal interpretation but at
the same time have many practical applications for today.

Where there are words or phrases in [brackets] within Scripture,
they have been inserted for clarification by the author.

Introduction

It was as though a veil had been removed from my eyes one extraordinary day, as I was made aware of the fact that my vision had actually been clouded for thirty-eight years. Immediately, things were revealed to me that I'd never allowed myself to see before, though I considered myself to be an open-minded person. How open-minded had I really been?

In June 1983, on that warm, sunny afternoon in my back yard, I was reading a book from a Christian friend. Since I wasn't a Christian at the time, it wasn't the type of book I would have chosen to read. Normally I would have put it down in disgust after reading the first few convicting pages; but on that particular day, I was compelled to open my mind, and because I did, my heart was opened to a miracle.

These simple poems, prayers, and promises are my testimony to you—a testimony to the Truth I never allowed myself to accept when it was given to me by others, because it made me uncomfortable. It always hit a nerve. Whenever I heard it, I didn't like the Truth, so I rejected it and sought false truths I felt much more comfortable with.

My most joyous work, in partnership with my Savior for the last 25 years, has been to write these simple, autobiographical poems as I have grappled with the circumstances of my life, and learned lessons I've needed to learn, with my Savior always present, giving me His constant truth to help me along the way through His Word. What I have written is now in your hands for a reason. You can read it or put it down and walk away. You have nothing to lose, and perhaps everything to gain.

I challenge you to read with your mind and heart open, not to something new, but to something renewing, that has always been, and always will be, the Truth.

The Truth will still be the Truth, whether you believe it or not.

Faithfully, Judith Doxey (another branch on the tree)

Acknowledgements

My deep gratitude goes to those who helped me see this book to completion in an all-out effort to see that God's work was done. You have also been tools in the hand of the Carpenter. "How beautiful are the feet of those who bring good news." (Romans 10:15).

I thank you, my amazing, valiant, and devoted family: Gene, Gia, Jared, Tim, Olivia, Sierra, Skylar, Alex, and Randy. I'm so thankful that you know and love God as I do. You are all answered prayer, my shining stars and my inspiration. To know we will all be together in eternity someday is an awesome tribute to God's mercy, forgiveness, and love.

Thank you, Candy Fiddes, dear friend, for praying and persevering in your witness to me, twenty-five years ago. That one book out of many you gave me finally made the impact God wanted, and opened my mind to Jesus.

Thank you, Mr. & Mrs. Carl Carlburg, for the *Strong's Concordance* (1890) that "went through the flood," as you had warned, and for your help in the beginning.

Thank you, Steve Gannon (K-Love Radio), for your hard advice, direction, and encouragement.

Thank you, Geoff Pope, for the skillful and encouraging editing I needed and prayed for. You were definitely answered prayer.

Thank you, Judy Nachazel, and Jon and Charlotte Mckee, for proofreading, and like all my precious friends, for being patient with me while I was so focused on getting this book done.

In Memory of:
My daughter, Justine Marie Doxey
My dad, Woody Hass
My friend, Linda Gabany

Table of Contents

This Book Is for You

This book I write for You, Father above,
In thanksgiving, in honor,
In worship and in love.
You've given me peace
And joy beyond measure.
I give You my life
And my work, with pleasure.

1 Corinthians 15:58b – "Always give yourselves to the work of the Lord, because you know your labor in the Lord is not in vain."

John 14:27 – "Peace I leave, My peace I give you."

Matthew 6:19-21 – "Do not store up for yourselves treasures on earth where moth and rust destroy, and where thieves break in and steal. But store up for yourselves treasures in heaven, where moth and rust do not destroy, and where thieves do not break in and steal. For where your treasure is, there your heart will be also."

Colossians 3:17 – "And whatever you do, whether in word or deed, do it all in the name of the Lord Jesus, giving thanks to God the Father through Him."

Listen In

I pray a lot throughout the day—
Conversations that are two-way.
In some of my poems that's what you'll see:
Me talking to God, and God talking to me.
So read the scriptures: that's the best part—
God speaking directly into my heart.
I invite you to listen in,
So you, too, can hear the truth from Him.

Matthew 11:16 (NKJV) "And blessed is he who is not offended because of Me"

Ready to Hear?

These words I've put on paper
Were written because they're true,
And it's no coincidence
They found their way to you.

Isaiah 30:8 – "Go now, write it on a tablet for them, inscribe it on a scroll, that for the days to come it may be an everlasting witness."

Holding Back the Truth

Why is it that I hesitate
To pass along the greatest news,
The best news one can ever hear?
My reasons why, I can't excuse.
Lord help me do the very thing
You want so much for me to do:
To tell others about Your truth,
And how they can get to know You.

There's a tension in Your message,
The saving truth that must be told;
And the silence that must be broken—
Oh, Lord, teach me to be so bold!
I hate my own guilty silence,
Knowing I have so much to say,
Yet holding back the very truth
From the ones for whom I pray.
For it opens a door to conflict
And people making fun of me.
It brings out their worst defenses,
For it's with YOU they disagree.

It's You they are at odds with, Lord.
It's You they aren't accepting.
This is what I must remember
When I feel it's me they're rejecting.

John 12:43 – "For they loved praise from men more than praise from God."

Galatians 1:10 – "Am I now trying to win approval of men, or of God? Or am I trying to please men? If I were still trying to please men, I would not be a servant of Christ."

Read: 1 Peter 2:20b-21

His Word Has the Clout

Each poem is a piece of me,
Some wrung out of trials and tears;
But at the end of the words I write,
God's Word faithfully appears—
Giving me peace and solutions,
Helping me see and understand.
He just sorts it all out for me
With a lesson that's all in His plan.
He takes all the good and the bad things,
And for His purpose He works them out;
And though I pray He uses these poems,
It's His Word that has the clout!

Proverbs 30:5 – "Every word of God is flawless; He is a shield to those who take refuge in Him."

Proverbs 30:6 – "Do not add to His words, or He will rebuke you and prove you a liar."

Psalm 119:105 – "Your word is a lamp to my feet and a light for my path."

Psalm 119:130 – "The unfolding of your words gives light; it gives understanding to the simple."

Read: Psalm 119 (about God's word)

Visions

I've painted with brushes
and I've painted with words
struggling with visions
where light and shadow merge.
What spills from my heart
must find form and shape
to make its impression
before it's too late.

Psalm 45:1 – My heart is stirred by a noble theme as I recite my verses for the King: My tongue is the pen of a skillful writer.

Read: Acts 2:17-21, 18:9-10, and 20:24.

This I Owe

It's taken twenty-four years to write this book.
God wanted it to be done just right.
Some obstacles along the way
Have humbled me and given insight.
I feel unworthy of this task.
Who am I to be used this way?
But, if one person can be saved,
Or one lamb kept from going astray,
Then I am moved to write the words
That fill my heart and overflow.
My deepest prayers and praise.
For all God's given, this I owe.

Proverbs 16:3 – "Commit to the Lord whatever you do, and your plans will succeed."

Proverbs 11:30 – "...he who wins souls is wise."

John 6:27 – "Do not work for food that spoils, but for food that endures to eternal life, which the Son of Man will give you. On Him, God the Father has placed His seal of approval."

Study: The Parable of the Sower, Mark 4

It Begins
With An
Open Heart

Chapter One

Listen With the Heart

Though it's all been said
By others before,
It will be said again
By many more.
But if man would listen
With more than his ears,
He would be saved
From many lost years.

Psalm 95:8 – "Today, if you hear His voice, do not harden your hearts."

John 8:47 – "He who belongs to God hears what God says. The reason you do not hear is that you do not belong to God."

John 18:37 – "Everyone on the side of the truth listens to me."

Resistance to God

I had been so misinformed.
I was primed for resistance.
So my stubborn misconceptions
Are what kept God at a distance.

Psalm 46:10 – "Be still and know that I am God; I will be exalted among the nations, I will be exalted in the earth."

1 Peter 3:8 – "For Christ died for sins once for all, the righteous for the unrighteous, to bring you to God."

John 4:25 – The woman said, "I know the Messiah" (called Christ) "is coming. When He comes, He will explain everything to us." Then Jesus declared, "I who speak to you am He."

What Do We Know?

In this world we're bound up
In thinking so small.
We really can't accept the fact
There's something beyond the wall
We've built around us.

We can't connect outside ourselves
To a power larger than us.
Our stubborn egos won't accept,
We simply cannot trust
In an Almighty God.

And even worse, we think it's a myth
That God could have sent His Son
To deliver us out of this bondage we're in;
Our minds can't conceive it was done
To set us free.

We humans have a problem
In reasoning as we do.
Our reasons become excuses,
Justifications, as if we actually knew
All there is to know.

Isaiah 25:11-12 – "God will bring down their pride despite the cleverness of their hands. He will bring down your fortified walls and lay them low."

Ephesians 4:18 – "They are darkened in their understanding and separated from the life of God because of the ignorance that is in them due to the hardening of their hearts."

Proverbs 24:7 – "Wisdom is too high for a fool; in the assembly at the gate he has nothing to say."

Of This World

Chained to the physical world,
Locked into habits of emotion and mind.
Wrapped in wounded self-importance,
Competing for recognition of some kind.
Lost on roads assumed all must go,
Following maps designed by man.
Indulging in all the world can offer,
Mindlessly aborting the "original" plan.

Ecclesiastes 4:4 – "And I saw that all labor and all achievement spring from man's envy of his neighbor. This too is meaningless, a chasing after the wind."

1 John 5:4a – "...for everyone born of God overcomes the world."

1 John 4:5 – "They are from the world and therefore speak from the viewpoint of the world, and the world listens to them."

1 John 2:15-16 – "Do not love the world or anything in the world. If anyone loves the world, the love of the Father is not in him. For everything in the world—the cravings of sinful man, the lust of his eyes and the boasting of what he has and does—comes not from the Father but from the world."

John 8:23-24 – "But He continued, 'You are from below; I am from above. You are of this world; I am not of this world. I told you that you would die in your sins; if you do not believe that I am the One I claim to be, you will indeed die in your sins.'"

Turning Your Back

When your heart becomes hardened
By disappointment and strife,
It also becomes defensive
Whenever Jesus offers you life.
When He taps you on the shoulder
To remind you He is there,
You've locked the door so tightly
That you're not even aware
Of how imprisoned you are
By the barriers you've built,
That you've closed yourself down
With your burden of guilt
And your bitterness toward God,
Though He never left your side.
It's you turning your back on Him
And creating that divide.
You've isolated your soul.
You chase everything but Him;
Things that give you nothing,
Leaving a void within.
But He's still right there waiting
For that moment you let go,
When you finally let your guard down,
And say "Yes," instead of "No."

Isaiah 45:22 – "Turn to Me and be saved, all you ends of the earth; for I am God, and there is no other."

Luke 23:34 – "Jesus said, 'Father, forgive them, for they do not know what they are doing.'"

Thanks Anyway!

"That's fine for you," I heard myself say,
"But I don't NEED Jesus. Thanks anyway.
I'm great without Him. All is well.
I'm good enough to not go to hell."

I thought...
Is she inferring that I'm not good?
How could I be so misunderstood?
I'm not a murderer or a thief.
(As if I'd never given God any grief!)
To me, Jesus was a crutch for the weak.
I couldn't see myself as a Jesus freak!
My life was going just fine without Him.
Besides, I wasn't living in sin.
I had everything under control.
(But was I at peace in my soul?)
How dare she say I needed God's Son!
(And why was I feeling the need to run?
Why was my heart beating so fast
And my defenses up like in the past?)
Her "dogma" I really didn't want to hear.
Besides, she'd get over it in a year!
This must be a "phase" she's going through.
How can she believe this stuff is true?
I can't accept that I'm a "sinner."
I feel so embarrassed for her.

Mark 16:15 – "He said to them, 'Go into all the world and preach the good news to all creation.'"

1 Corinthians 1:18 – "For the message of the cross is foolishness to those who are perishing, but to us who are being saved it is the power of God."

Read: 1 Corinthians 2:14 and Ephesians 4:18

13

Something More

Who was that young woman
I left way back there
Who valued her life
But was also aware...
There had to be more?

Who was that little child,
Hiding inside that shell,
Playing a grown-up
Who couldn't act very well?
There had to be more.

She lived in the world,
A troublesome place,
Struggling so hard
To stay in the race.
There had to be more.

She didn't feel right
By the standards of man
And felt out of place
In the worldly plan...
There had to be more.

She felt something amiss,
Down deep in her soul,
And desperately sought
To keep herself whole.
There had to be more.

She was just part of an act
On this earthly stage,
Trapped by closed doors
Like a bird in a cage.
There had to be more.

Aching for freedom,
She sat down one day
And read about Jesus,
Then heard someone say,
"There is something more —
Just open the door."

Revelation 3:20 – "'If anyone hears my voice and opens the door, I will come into him and dine with him.'"

2 Corinthians 5:17 – "Therefore, if anyone is in Christ, he is a new creature; the old has gone and the new has come!"

John 15:16 – "'You did not choose Me, but I chose you to go out and bear fruit— fruit that will last.'"

Exposed

God was like a brilliant search-light,
Exposing my soul to Himself and to me.
All my excuses were revealed and laid open,
And I didn't like what I could see.
He illuminated deep corners of my being
As He showed me who I am.
My self-will and pride couldn't push Him away;
I could see that my life was a sham.
As the heat of His lamp was melting my past
And leading the old me away,
My heart opened up and softened to Him,
As I died and was reborn that day.

Proverbs 20:27 – "The lamp of the Lord searches the spirit of a man; it searches out his inmost being."

Ephesians 5:13 – "But everything exposed by the light becomes visible, for it is light that makes everything visible."

Day of Salvation

Something happened to me
As I was reading in the sun.
All words lack in meaning
For what had begun.
The heat of that day
Had nothing to do
With the warmth that entered
And made me brand new.
I was reading about how Jesus
Was dying just for me,
When a wall of darkness crumbled;
And for the first time, I could see.
I had opened my mind
To this book from a friend,
Then God opened my heart
And I let Him come in.
It happened so gently,
So silently He came;
And from that moment on,
I haven't been the same.
All my burdens lifted
When He freed me that day.
All guilt and pain and sorrow
Were completely washed away.

John 3:3 – "I tell you the truth, unless a man is born again, he cannot see the Kingdom of God."

Daniel 12:1b – "...everyone whose name is found written in the book—will be delivered."

John 16:13 – "But when He, the Spirit of Truth, comes, He will guide you into all truth."

Forgiven

Alone and seeking truth,
Not aware of Him,
I soon felt His presence,
The touching of a friend.
He held me but a moment
In His forgiving love,
Lifting high my sorry heart
To One who stood above.
He emptied me of everything,
Then filled me up again.
Tears of pain and then of joy
Flowed free because of Him.
He didn't tell me Who He was.
He didn't need to speak.
Such power in His presence,
And yet He was so meek.
So gentle and forgiving,
Embracing me with light,
Opening my blinded soul
And I receiving sight.

Silent as He came, He left—
"Oh, please, stay here with me!"
And as time passed, I heard Him
Where nothing used to be.
Unworthy and in need was I
Of His amazing Grace.
Then all I did was seek Him,
And through His Word I saw His face.
I hear His voice within me still.
He's never far away.
I feel His arms surrounding me
Throughout each new-born day.

1 Titus 1:15 – "Here is a trustworthy saying that deserves full acceptance: Christ Jesus came into the world to save sinners—of whom I am the worst."

Psalm 145:18-19 – "The Lord is near to all who call on Him, who call on Him in truth. He fulfills the desires of those who fear Him; He hears their cry and saves them."

One Regret

More than anything else
I'd like you to see
How I also resisted
So hard and stubbornly.
I regret that today,
Knowing now what I do,
I almost missed Jesus,
The One called Faithful and True.
Sure, I could have lived life;
I would have muddled through,
But hope would be missing,
And my true purpose, too.
No way would I turn back
To what I believed then,
As I've seen both sides now
And I'm not going back again.

Acts 20:24 – "However, I consider my life worth nothing to me, if only I may finish the race and complete the task the Lord Jesus has given me—the task of testifying to the gospel of God's grace."

Clueless

The moment I found Jesus
I realized I'd been lost—
That He'd been seeking me
At every road I crossed.
As I went my own sweet way
For, oh so many a year,
He hoped that I would notice
At some point that He was near.
No, I didn't even look,
So certain I knew the way—
So typical of the lost,
Clueless that they've gone astray.

Luke 19:10 – "'For the Son of Man came to seek and save the lost.'"

Luke 15:24 – "'For this son of mine was dead and is alive again; he was lost and is found.' So they began to celebrate."

Read: Luke 15:3-7; Jeremiah 50:6-7

Wash the Windows!

My windows were once blurry and dingy,
Though I was convinced I could see just fine.
To think I could have lived my entire life
Not seeing what's real because of the grime!
But one day I was called to awaken
By a splendid clarity and range of light.
Did somebody wash the windows, or what?
'Cuz the difference was like day and night!
What I see now I couldn't see before,
Though these things had been there all along.
So many think their windows aren't dirty;
They think they see clearly, but they're wrong.
It's a hard thing to convince someone
That what they see is clouded by grime;
But until they, too, get their windows washed,
They'll continue to think what they see is just fine.

Matthew 13:16-17 – "'But blessed are your eyes because they see, and your ears because they hear. For I tell you the truth, many prophets and righteous men longed to see what you see but did not see it, and to hear what you hear but did not hear it.'"

2 Corinthians 4:18 – "So we fix our eyes not on what is seen, but on what is unseen. For what is seen is temporary, but what is unseen is eternal."

Another Reminder

What a thrill as I watch
The lightning crack the sky,
And feel the thunder rumble
Like fireworks to a child's eye.
My dog runs frightened to me
And sits shaking at my feet,
As the rain begins to shower us,
Washing away the summer heat.
I close my eyes and listen,
Breathe deep, and quietly sit.
With awesome wonder God declares
His proven power above it.
Another clear reminder,
As God signals He's still near,
Commanding our attention...
How can anyone not hear?

Matthew 11:15 – "'He who has ears, let him hear.'"

John 8:47 – "He who belongs to God hears what God says. The reason you do not hear is that you do not belong to God.'"

Psalm 19:1 – "The heavens declare the glory of God; the skies proclaim the work of His hands."

The Highest Honor

Oh joy! Oh rapture!
Oh wonder divine!
To walk in the beauty
Of God's perfect design!
To breathe in real life.
To witness His grace.
To be in His presence
And feel His embrace!
To be wrapped in His love
And know Him as Friend
Is the highest honor
One can comprehend!
It's simply awesome
To see through His eyes,
His wondrous creation
And all it supplies!
I feel so welcomed,
So completed in Him,
That I just can't lose...
I can only win!

Psalm 34:5 – "Those who look to Him are radiant; their faces are never covered in shame."

Psalm 26:8 – "I love the house where You live, O Lord, the place where Your glory dwells."

Psalm 28:6-7 – "Praise be to the Lord, for He has heard my cry for mercy. The Lord is my strength and my shield; my heart trusts in Him, and I am helped. My heart leaps for joy and I will give thanks to Him in song."

Children of the King

Listen very carefully,
My dearest ones,
My precious children,
My cherished daughters and sons:
Do not run away from Me.
I am your Father, the King.
You can trust Me with your life;
You can trust Me for everything.
I want the very best for you
And great purpose for your life.
All I ask of you is love.
Let me show you wrong from right.
You can talk to me anytime,
But you must listen, too.
The world won't have the answers.
I will never lie to you.

Love, Your Heavenly Father

Hebrews 6:18 – "...it is impossible for God to lie...."

Numbers 23:19 – "'God is not a man that He should lie, nor a son of man that he should change His mind. Does He speak and then not act? Does He promise and not fulfill?'"

Isaiah 45:19b – "'I, the Lord, speak the truth; I declare what is right.'"

The Humbling Process

Chapter Two

The Narrow Gate

I wandered so many garden paths
That were traveled by others like me;
Some circled through forests and flowering fields,
And several led straight to the sea.
Wherever I ventured I saw a small gate
Nestled quietly off to the side,
Narrow and white and slightly ajar,
But always, I'd pass it in stride.
Most walked by as a few stepped through,
But it seemed too narrow for me.
That little gate seemed more like an end,
And there was so much more I had to see.
I met a few people who'd been through that gate,
And they tried to convince me to enter;
But I couldn't accept how important it was
That this gate should become their center.
So I continued to walk other ways,
Taking wide paths that large crowds poured through;
But when I followed those same wide paths,
There were more paths the big ones led into.
Confused and tired of the same winding trails,
I looked toward the white, narrow gate.
I stood in wonder at its simple appearance,
Its humble, unassuming state.

When I felt drawn to go near it,
I stood silently within an amazing peace.
Then I found myself stepping through
And I knew my seeking had ceased.
When I finally had seen the other side,
I was sorry for my ignorant years.
If I'd listened and opened my eyes before,
I wouldn't have known such tears.
Now I know I must go back again
To tell everyone what I've seen.
Though it hurts that most people won't listen,
I know it's all part of God's scheme.

Matthew 7:13 – "'Enter through the narrow gate. For wide is the gate and broad is the road that leads to destruction, and many enter through it. But small is the gate and narrow the road that leads to life, and only a few find it."

John 10:9 – "'I am the gate; whoever enters through me will be saved.'"

Catalysts

Unexplainable things happen
In everyone's life:
Overpowering moments
Or long periods of strife —
Events that test our strength
Or over-run our senses,
That may introduce us to pain,
Or bring up our worst defenses.
It may cause us to question God,
Or the very reason we exist,
Leading us to soul-search
Or to push and fight and resist.
We can go into denial
Or blame everyone around,
Or see it as the gift it is —
A catalyst to the profound.
Sometimes we need to be shaken,
The rug pulled out from under us.
We need to be awakened,
Though it might seem unjust.
But God needs our attention,
And so He allows these things to be —
Whatever it takes to reach us,
It seems we just don't make it easy.

Isaiah 2:63 – "You will keep in perfect peace him whose mind is steadfast, because he trusts in You."

Colossians 3:2 – "Set your mind on things above, not on earthly things."

Job 23:10 – "But He knows the way that I take; when He has tested me, I shall come forth as gold."

For Justine's Sake

God sent us an angel one bright April day,
But because she was fragile, she couldn't stay.
She had been with the Father before she came here,
For whenever we held her, we'd feel Him near.
Each time she smiled, God shown from her face,
As her tiny heart entrusted special love on this place.
But not till years later did we understand
How through her life here, God extended His hand.
He opened up our souls and uncovered our eyes,
As we shared in her parting with painful good-byes.
We gave up our angel back into God's care,
But in His sacrifice to us, ours could never compare.
Through our beloved child His reason was willed;
And for Justine's sake, her purpose fulfilled.
For we now know the Father, and Jesus, His Son,
And because of two lives—our salvation was won.

Hebrews 13:2 – "Do not forget to entertain strangers; for by so doing some people have entertained angels without knowing it."

Romans 8:28 – "And we know that in all things God works for the good of those who love Him, who have been called according to His purpose."

Job 23:10 – "But He knows the way that I take; when He has tested me, I will come forth as gold."

Proverbs 16:4 – "The Lord works out everything for His own ends…."

One Last Time

I held her tightly
One last time
And felt the stillness
Of her tiny heart
Against the aching of mine.

April 14, 1976 – November 3, 1977

John 11:35 – "Jesus wept."

God's Nudge

Sometimes it's the worst thing
That happens as we live,
That opens the door
To the best God has to give.
A blessing or a curse?
Don't be too quick to judge.
What your circumstances are
May simply be God's nudge.

Romans 8:28 – "And we know that in all things God works for the good of those who love Him, who have been called according to His purpose."

Read: The Book of Ruth

Now I Have an Open Line

There were times I prayed endlessly,
Pleading for God's ear—
Begging for some mercy,
Wanting to feel Him near.
Those days of lonely crying,
Of feeling apart from Him,
Made me more an unbeliever
While my hopes grew very dim.
Why couldn't I reach Him?
Was He even there?
An empty silence followed
After each unanswered prayer.
Finally, I just gave up.
My world had fallen apart.
I had begged Him for some mercy,
And yet He broke my heart.
But, seven years later,
The key was given to me.
It opened up the way to God
So I could finally see—
That God had been there all along,
But I couldn't hear His voice,
For I hadn't accepted Jesus;
I hadn't made "The Choice."

God had tried to reach me, too.
It hurt Him to see me cry.
He suffered as well, while I held my child,
Watching her slowly die.
If I had only known back then
That Jesus was the Key,
I would have heard God's answers then;
They would have lifted me.
But now I have an open line;
God answers all my calls,
For Jesus Christ, His only Son,
Broke down my self-built walls.

1 Timothy 2:5 – "For there is one God and one mediator between God and man, the man Christ Jesus."

Where Sorrow Leads

Those years of my life
That were full of pain,
That took something from me,
Were replaced with gain.

The battles I fought
And also lost
Gave much more back
And were worth the cost.

All trials that hurt me
Are turning points;
They bring me nearer—
Each one anoints.

Each fear brings faith,
Each mystery, peace;
Each question an answer,
Each truth a release.

God shares my sorrows.
He gives me rest.
He makes me keep growing.
I'm truly blest!

Job 12:10 – "'When He hath tried me, I shall come forth as gold.'"

Ecclesiastes 7:3 – "Sorrow is better than laughter; for by the sadness of the countenance the heart is made better."

2 Corinthians 7:9 – "Yet now I am happy, not because you were made sorry, but because your sorrow led you to repentance. For you became sorrowful as God intended."

Don't Waste Your Sorrows

Don't waste your sorrows
On self pity or blame.
Don't give in to bitterness,
Guilt or complaint.

Those who do suffer
While here on earth
Can someday reign
And know their true worth.

But some avoid suffering;
They don't want pain.
So they hold back from life
And their hearts grow lame.

Find what sorrow gives you
And use it to grow.
Transform it into lessons
God wants you to know.

James 1:2-4 – "Consider it pure joy, my brothers, whenever you face trials of many kinds, because you know that the testing of your faith develops perseverance. Perseverance must finish its work so that you may be mature and complete, not lacking anything."

Compensated

Things happened to me
that were out of my control.
Many times I was hurt by them
when life took its toll.
But I've been compensated now
for all my broken dreams.
I've even been rewarded
beyond all worldly means.
No matter what happens here,
I know I cannot lose.
I am on the winning team
because Jesus paid my dues.

Romans 8:18 – "Our present sufferings are not worth comparing with the glory that will be revealed in us."

1 John 5:4 – "For everyone born of God overcomes the world. This is the victory that has overcome the world, even our faith."

Curses Transformed to Gifts

All that bad stuff that happens
When we feel our life is cursed,
When we are protesting God
And our faith is at its worst—
We have to know down the road
That God's good will be revealed—
The curse gives birth to a gift;
An abundance it will yield.
In every challenge of life
We must learn to look ahead,
Beyond what we now protest
To God's intended gift instead.

Romans 8:28 – "And we know that in all things God works for the good of those who love Him, and who have been called according to His purpose."

Romans 5:3-5 – "Not only so, but we also rejoice in our sufferings, because we know that suffering produces perseverance; perseverance, character; and character, hope. And hope does not disappoint us, because God has poured out His love into our hearts by the Holy Spirit, whom He has given us."

Ready to Be Used

It's our desert experiences
that truly make us humble,
that keep our pride in check
when our ego takes a tumble.
If we have to reach out for help,
or step down off our ladder,
to see we're nothing without God,
then our selfish motives shatter.
When we're little in our own eyes,
only then are we ready
and able to live on God's terms,
so He can use us sure and steady.

Numbers 12:3 – "Now Moses was a very humble man, more humble than anyone else on the face of the earth.

Samuel 15:17 – "Samuel said, 'Although you were once small in your own eyes, did you not become the head of the tribes of Israel? The Lord anointed you king over Israel.'"

Identity

It isn't in our titles here,
In our degrees or awards,
In people applauding us,
Or our trips to distant shores.
It isn't the country we come from,
Or the religions we create,
The color of our skin or hair
Or whether we're simple or great.
It isn't in whom we marry
Or the politics we choose.
It isn't in the way we look
Or in the products we use.
It isn't in our careers
Or how we spend free time,
Or how much money we have,
In the stars or in our sign.
It isn't in our children,
Or the homes and cars we own—
No. We won't find our identity,
Except in God alone.

Study: Jeremiah 10:23

Colossians 3:2 – "Set your minds on things above, not on earthly things."

Psalm 3:20 – "But our citizenship is in heaven. And we eagerly await a Savior from there, the Lord Jesus Christ."

1 John 2:16 – "For everything in the world—the cravings of sinful man, the lust of his eyes, and the boasting of what he has and does—comes not from the Father but from the world.

What Goes Up Must Come Down

Humility grows in the valleys
of selflessness and sacrifice,
Not up on the peaks of pride
where some try to stay at any price.
It's only a matter of time
before what goes up must come down.
Those mountaintops get cold and lonely,
where only an echo of self resounds.

Matthew 23:12 – "'For whoever exalts himself will be humbled, and whoever humbles himself will be exalted.'"

Proverbs 11:2 – "When pride comes, then comes disgrace, but with humility comes wisdom."

Philippians 2:3-4 – "Do nothing out of selfish ambition or vain conceit, but in humility consider others better than yourselves. Each of you should look not only to your own interests, but to the interests of others."

Read: Philippians 2:1-18; Titus 3:1-2; 1 Peter 5:1-6

On-The-Job-Training

I'm in training for heaven
as a born-again child.
My tribulations here
have not been mild.
This is my classroom
here on earth,
where my Master teaches
and gives new birth.
He shapes me through brokenness
and Agape (Love).
It's on-the-job-training
that is graded above.
Character development
through blessed sorrow
makes me sometimes wish
graduation were tomorrow.

Job 5:7 – "Blessed is the man whom God corrects; so do not despise the discipline of the Almighty."

Proverbs 12:1 – "Whoever loves discipline loves knowledge, but whoever hates correction is stupid."

2 Timothy 4:7 – "I have fought the good fight, I have finished the race, I have kept the faith. Now there is in store for me the crown of righteousness, which the Lord, the Righteous Judge, will award me on that day."

Not Mine But His

When I receive my crown in heaven,
Though considered to be my reward,
There's no way I will have earned it,
When all I did was trust in the Lord.
So when I find myself in heaven,
And God places that crown on my head,
I'll take it and place it at His feet,
Giving Him all the glory instead.

Revelation 4:10b-11a – "They lay their crowns before the throne and say, 'You are worthy our Lord and God, to receive glory and honor and power....'"

Study: Revelation Chapter 4

Facing The Truth

Chapter Three

Dear Lord,

How can I tell them
What they don't want to see?
Even when it's Your truth
That can set them free?

My Child,

Tell them anyway,
Then leave the rest to Me,
For your efforts are rewarded
In eternity.

Isaiah 55:11 – "'...so is my word that goes out from my mouth. It will not return to me empty, but will accomplish what I desire and achieve the purpose for which I sent it.'"

Matthew 23:28 (NKJV) "And blessed is he who is not offended because of Me."

The Wolf Among Us

Where there is no Shepherd,
The wolf moves into the flock,
Slowly easing his way in,
Calmly, so as not to shock.
He sits among them while they graze,
Pretending he's no threat,
Until they become used to him,
So the closer he can get.
Deceptively cool and cunning,
He quietly makes his advance,
Until he goes unnoticed,
And that's when he sees his chance.
As he springs into action
And grabs the closest one,
The flock begins reacting
As they scatter about or run.
The wolf drags his prize away,
As he's done many times before;
You'd think the sheep would know by now,
But he continues to steal more.

John 10:10 – "'The thief comes only to steal and kill and destroy; I have come that they may have life, and have it to the full.'"

Acts 20:29-31a – I know that after I leave, savage wolves will come in among you and will not spare the flock. Even from your own number men will arise and distort the truth in order to draw away disciples after them. So be on your guard!

Cloak of Anonymity

Satan is alive and well,
Clapping his hands in glee.
He's doing his best work under
The cloak of anonymity.
If we don't believe he's real,
That makes him happy as can be.
That's how he's able to attack
Our areas of vulnerability.

2 Corinthians 11:14 – "And no wonder, for Satan himself masquerades as an angel of light."

Lies Based on Truth

Woven within the woolen tapestry of truth
Winds a lovely strand of gold,
More brilliantly visible than the wool
And more luminous to behold.
It shamelessly weaves among the threads,
Seeking only to deface,
By masking truth it labors to hide
While leaving its golden trace.
Adding to the woolen tapestry of truth
Its own deceptive lines,
It often succeeds in covering the truth
Behind its golden designs.
The woolen truth, though steadfast,
Is the fiber and strength for the gold,
Though the glistening strand takes away and adds
To the truth the tapestry holds.

Psalm 4:2 – "How long, O men, will you turn my glory into shame? How long will you love delusions and seek false gods?"

Revelation 22:18-19 – "I warn everyone who hears the words of this prophesy of this book [the Bible]: If anyone adds anything to them, God will add to him the plagues described in this book. And if anyone takes words away from this book of prophesy [leaves anything out], God will take away from him his share in the tree of life and in the holy city, which are described in this book."

(Words in [brackets] are mine for clarification)

Comfortable with Evil

Slowly making an appearance,
It showed itself in little ways,
Helping the world get comfortable,
At times making bold displays.
We've slowly become accustomed,
No longer embarrassed or shocked,
And now we see the tables turned—
As what is good and right is mocked.

Jeremiah 11:7-8 – "I warned them again and again, saying, 'Obey me.' But they did not listen or pay attention; instead, they followed the stubbornness of their evil hearts."

Isaiah 30:9-11 – "These are rebellious people, deceitful children unwilling to listen to the Lord's instruction. They say to the seers, 'See no more visions!' And to the prophets, 'Give us no more visions of what is right! Tell us pleasant things, prophesy illusions. Leave this way, get off this path, and stop confronting us with the Holy One of Israel!'"

Read: 2 Thessalonians 2:7-12

True Wisdom

Placing God at the center
Of one's quest for truth is wise.
By comprehending who He is,
We see reality through His eyes.
God is the beginning of wisdom;
Without Him we cannot understand.
Lifelong learning through believing
And true wisdom go hand in hand.

Proverbs 9:10 – The fear of the Lord is the beginning of wisdom, and knowledge of the Holy One is understanding.

Read: Proverbs 8:32-36

1 Corinthians 2:8 – None of the rulers of this age understood it, for if they had, they would not have crucified the Lord of glory.

The Simple Truth

The truth is far too simple
For some to understand.
The truth is also narrow,
And it just will not expand.
Though many try to stretch it
(Adding and taking away),
God's the One Who made the truth
The same today as yesterday.
If truth is truth, it cannot change,
And its Author stays the same;
But man keeps trying anyway
To modify it in vain.
We might not like the truth much;
With it we may disagree.
But it does no good to fight the truth;
Once we accept it, then we see.

Revelation 22:18-20 – "I warn everyone who hears the prophecy of this book: If anyone adds anything to them, God will add to him the plagues described in this book. And if anyone takes words away from this book of prophecy, God will take away from him his share in the tree of life and in the holy city, which are described in this book. He who testifies to these things says, 'Yes, I am coming soon.'"

Crooked or Straight

If you lay a crooked stick
With crooked sticks all around,
It may not seem so crooked,
Until you lay a straight one down.

Proverbs 13:20 – He who walks with the wise grows wise, but a companion of fools suffers harm.

Titus 1:15 – To the pure, all things are pure, but to those who are corrupted and do not believe, nothing is pure.

Jude 4 – For certain men whose condemnation was written about long ago have secretly slipped in among you. They are godless men, who change the grace of our God into a license for immorality and deny Jesus Christ our only sovereign and Lord.

In the Midst of It All

It's getting harder and harder
To find Jesus in all of this;
In the midst of worldly chaos,
His quiet voice we seem to miss.
We get drawn into the world
With its terror and wars
And the many catastrophes
That are happening more and more.
But that's the way Satan likes it,
Disrupting our lives every day.
He wants to keep us distracted
So he can keep leading us away
From the One we need to see and hear,
Right in the middle of it all,
Who's standing smack in front of us,
Waiting for us to heed His call.

2 Corinthians 4:4 – The god of this age [Satan] has blinded the minds of unbelievers, so that they cannot see the light of the gospel of the glory of Christ, who is the image of God.

1 John 5:5 – Who is it that overcomes the world? Only he who believes that Jesus is the Son of God.

Isaiah 55:2-3 – "'Why spend money on what is not bread, and your labor on what does not satisfy? Listen, listen to Me, and eat what is good, and your soul will delight in the richest of fare. Give ear and come to Me, that your soul may live.'"

Genesis 28:16 – When Jacob awoke from his sleep, he thought, "Surely the Lord is in this place, and I was not aware of it."

Convicted

I can talk about religions,
And nobody gets upset.
Saying "Buddha" or "Mohammed"
Seems to pose no threat.
I can speak of Confucius or Gandhi,
Simple prophets from the past.
But let me speak of "Jesus"
And all present seem aghast!
What is it about His name
That unravels people so?
Why does the name of Jesus
Cause many to turn and go?

No others claimed to be God,
As Jesus claimed to be;
That made Him more than others,
The Messiah of prophecy.
He proved more than a prophet
He was the "anointed" One,
Crucified for who He was,
Not for what He had done.

And what did He really do?
He revealed His Father's perfect grace.
So when "Jesus" is spoken now,
Man runs and hides his face.

John 10:30 – "I and the Father are one."

John 12:44-45 – Then Jesus cried out, "When a man believes in me, he does not believe in me only, but in the One who sent me. When he looks at me, he sees the One who sent me."

John 14:10 – "Don't you believe that I am in the Father, and that the Father is in Me? The words I say to you are not just My own. Rather, it is the Father, living in Me, who is doing His work."

The Annoying Truth

You want that "feel good" religion,
With prosperity and peace.
You want only validations
And no words to cause you grief.
You say:

"Tell me what I want to hear,
Not what I need to know.
Don't offend me with the truth
Or I'll just turn and go."

But you know God is speaking to you
When your heart pounds and you squirm.
God's truth is often hard to hear,
But how else will you learn?
Pretty sermons will not save you.
Feeling good won't make you whole.
And doing nice things for others
Simply will not save your soul.

So when God is really speaking
And says, "Listen to my Son,"
You have to hear what Jesus says.
It's through Him God's truth comes.
Yes. Jesus is the answer,
The truth that you avoid,
The One you keep hearing about
When you feel the most annoyed!

God's truth is clear and constant;
It will always be the same,
And He'll follow you everywhere,
Whispering His Son's name.
For it's only in the name of Jesus
That eternal life is yours;
And God won't stop telling you this,
Because Jesus is Heaven's door.

Hebrews 1:2 – ...but in these last days he has spoken to us by His Son, whom He appointed heir of all things, and through whom He made the universe.

Read: Isaiah 30:9-11 and Hebrews 1, 2, and 3.

It's Not What We Think

We're looking in all the wrong places,
Hearing only what we want to hear,
Seeking the answers that fit our lives now,
Though our lives may change in a year.
We avoid the truth we are looking for,
Because it's not what we think it should be.
Whenever the truth stands before us,
It shows us our sin, so we flee.

Romans 6:23 – For the wages of sin is death, but the gift of God is eternal life in Christ Jesus our Lord.

Romans 3:22 – This righteousness from God comes through faith in Jesus Christ to all who believe. There is no difference, for all have sinned and fall short of the glory of God.

1 John 1:8 – If we claim to be without sin, we deceive ourselves and the truth is not in us.

Religion Is Not the Answer—
Salvation Is

Religions
come from the world.
Jesus Christ
came from above.
Religions
begin in the minds of men.
Jesus Christ
began in God.

Colossians 2:8 – See to it that no one takes you captive through hollow and deceptive philosophy, which depends on human tradition and the basic principles of this world rather than on Christ.

Matthew 15:8-9 – "These people honor Me with their lips, but their hearts are far from Me. They worship Me in vain; their teachings are but rules taught by man."

The Body of Christ

God's church is not a religion;
It's not a building or place.
It's simply those who know Jesus,
Believers saved by God's grace.
With Jesus as the head of them,
They are His body in motion,
Doing the work He has given them,
Sharing His word and devotion.

Ephesians 1:22-23 – And God placed all things under His [Jesus'] feet and appointed Him to be head over everything for the church, which is His body, the fullness of Him who fills everything in every way.

Ephesians 4:15-16 – Instead, speaking the word in love, we will in all things grow up into Him who is the Head, that is, Christ. From Him the whole body, joined and held together by every supporting ligament, grows and builds itself up in love, as each part does its work.

Read: Ephesians 5:28-30

The Name No Christian Would Deny

I hear people say they are Christians,
Just because they may believe in God;
Yet they don't believe who Jesus is,
So are they Christians, or not?
It's in the very word, "Christian,"
Where I think the answer lies:
For the first part, "Christ" is Jesus,
The name no Christian would deny.
Christ is Jesus, God in the flesh;
A true Christian believes in Him.
So belief in God, but not His Son,
Is an absolute contradiction.

John 5:23b – "He who does not honor the Son does not honor the Father, who sent Him."

John 6:29 – Jesus answered, "The work of God is to believe in the One He has sent."

1 John 4:15 – If anyone acknowledges that Jesus is the Son of God, God lives in him and he in God.

I John 2:22-23 – Who is the liar? It is the man who denies that Jesus is the Christ. Such a man is the antichrist—he denies the Father and the Son. No one who denies the Son has the Father; whoever acknowledges the Son has the Father also.

Burden of Sin

In thought or word or deed,
Sin's guilt will hold you down.
It can be oppressive
And its effect profound.

You can
Not think about your sin,
Just blow it off each day,
Ignore the mopping up you do
And keep on running away—
Or just get used to it
As its weight increases,
Slowing your life down,
Or crushing it to pieces.
Maybe, try not to notice
How it affects others:
Your spouse and your children,
Your sisters and your brothers.

Or you can
Simply deal with it.
Confess your sin and repent.
The burden will be lifted
And beneath you'll find content.
Jesus wants to free you
From your self-built prison.

Or you can keep your life locked up;
Make your own decision.

Acts 2:21 – And everyone who calls on the name of the Lord will be saved.

Acts 2:40 – With many other words he warned them; and he pleaded with them, "Save yourselves from this corrupt generation."

Psalm 106:43 – Many times He delivered them, but they were bent on rebellion and they wasted away in their sin.

Read: Acts 2:38, Acts 3:19 and Acts 10:43

Paradox

The Gospel seems a paradox.
It goes against all common "sense."
It contradicts man's logic,
With its supernatural events.
Man just cannot accept the truth
Until he surrenders his own.
It's in one humble moment
This revelation can be known.
But man tries to design his own truth
So it fits into his worldly ways,
Then farther from the real truth,
And himself, he then strays.

1 John 2:22 – Who is the liar? It is the man who denies that Jesus Christ is the Christ.

Isaiah 55:8 – For my thoughts are not your thoughts, neither are your ways my ways.

1 Corinthians 1:19-20 – "I will destroy the wisdom of the wise, the intelligence of the intelligent I will frustrate." Where is the wise man? Where is the scholar? Where is the philosopher of this age? Has not God made foolish the wisdom of the world?

Read: 2 Timothy 4:3-4

Sheep Without a Shepherd

Like sheep without a shepherd,
They are helpless and lost;
Harassed and hopeless,
By every storm they're tossed.
Paralyzed by the darkness,
Unable to see the way,
With no shepherd's voice leading,
Each turn leads them astray.
They simply are not grounded
And cannot see their plight,
Even though they move in circles
And are frightened in the night.
They can run right into danger
With no shepherd to protect.
Exposed to all deceptive calls,
No evil can they detect.
No peace can they ever know
Without the shepherd near
To keep them safe and lead them
To a place of no more fear.

Matthew 9:36 – When He saw the crowds, He had compassion on them, because they were harassed and helpless, like sheep without a shepherd.

Matthew 12:30 – "He who is not with me is against Me, and he who does not gather with Me scatters."

Read: Ezekiel 34:5, 11-16

The Shepherd Story

A Lesson in Overcoming Stubbornness and Grief

John 8:47 – "He who belongs to God hears what God says. The reason you do not hear is that you do not belong to God."

Picture in your mind a shepherd of old, trying to lead his sheep, with their young lambs, out from the high mountain meadows where they have been grazing all summer long. He wants to lead them to the lush, valley pastures below before the winter snows come. As a wise shepherd, he knows that the sheep will either starve or freeze to death if they stay much longer where they are. He knows well the only path that will take the sheep down the steep, narrow and craggy mountainside.

Some of the sheep want to stay where they are. They don't know what the shepherd knows. They are content with filling their bellies and don't want to follow the shepherd to a place they can't see. They can't understand why they should leave such a seemingly perfect place.

Nevertheless, the shepherd begins the process of moving his flock, and the sheep that trust him respond to his calls and prompting. Some of the sheep recall from past experience that the shepherd knows the way to go and what is best for them, because they have followed him before. They remember that the journey is worth the effort. They know what awaits them, so they put their faith in the shepherd, even though the path he leads them on is not always easy. Though the way can sometimes be difficult, they know as long as they do exactly what he says, he will get them to their home down in the pleasant pastures of the valley.

Those sheep that are being stubborn and don't want to go are wandering off their own ways, grazing where they please and ignoring the shepherd's calls. But the shepherd doesn't give up on them. He tries lots of different things to get them to follow him.

He is always calling to them, using special words and sounds to try to keep them focused on him. Sometimes he uses his large staff to point the way or to snatch them away from danger. Other times he may use a rod to physically guide or steer them with gentle prodding from behind or on their sides. Sometimes he has to leave the flock to go find those that have wandered off and gotten lost. Often the shepherd will bring another sheep alongside of a stubborn one to help lead it towards him. Sometimes the shepherd has to take more drastic measures when nothing else works, yet there will still be those that refuse to follow, and, sadly, they will die when the freezing snows come to the high meadows.

One of the more drastic measures the shepherd has been known to use may seem cruel to those who cannot see the whole picture or understand his loving purpose.

Picture again the shepherd walking among a small family of stubborn sheep who refuse to follow him. Without warning, he snatches up one of their tiny lambs in his arms and walks away with it—and begins the journey down the mountain without them. You can imagine the commotion it causes. The mother of the lamb becomes frantic and cries out for her baby, but to no avail. The father of the lamb runs around aggressively, but nothing he does brings the baby back to them. They don't understand what has happened, or why. They feel helpless and are left behind to struggle with their loss.

Meanwhile, in the distant reaches of the mountain, heading down the steep path to the valley below, the shepherd leads the rest of his flock. He carries in his arms the little sleeping lamb as he continues to call back to the stubborn sheep who are still grieving, confused, and wondering why the shepherd took their little lamb from them.

Will the stubborn sheep that are left behind finally choose to follow the shepherd and therefore see their baby again, or will they choose to stay where they are and die? Who will they trust: themselves or the shepherd?

For thirty-eight years of my life, I was one of those stubborn sheep who didn't want to follow the Shepherd, Jesus Christ. Though there were times, as I look back, when I heard Him calling to me, I didn't think I needed Him. I thought I was doing just fine on my own. It looked to me like I had everything I needed, so there seemed no reason why I should follow this "Shepherd" I'd heard and read about most of my life. Why would anyone want to leave all they'd ever known for a place they'd never seen? Did this place really exist?

I thought Jesus Christ, was only for those who were weak or narrow-minded, naive or brainwashed, ignorant, or were really, really bad people called "sinners." I felt I was above all that stuff. I was a "good" person. I was better than that. I was smarter than that. I didn't need "saving." The world and all it had to offer seemed good enough for me, just like those high, lush, mountain meadows seemed good enough for those stubborn sheep. I didn't know what the Shepherd knew. I couldn't see up ahead. I wasn't able to see something better than what I already had. I only saw a very small part of the whole picture.

I remember times when the Shepherd sent other sheep to come alongside me, to encourage me to listen, and respond to his calls. I also remember how offended I felt whenever those believers spoke to me about Jesus Christ. I thought they were telling me that I wasn't a good person. I felt I was good, and that would get me into heaven, if there was a heaven. So why would I need Jesus? How dare they imply that I needed something more. To me, that meant I wasn't good enough the way I was. So I was on the defense.

I'm sure those stubborn sheep up there on the mountain in those beautiful meadows were good sheep. They were, more than likely, good parents, good sons and daughters, and good friends and neighbors. They probably took a lot of pride in that. I know I was prideful about my family and my way of life. Looking back, that pride was probably what kept me from responding to the Shepherd's calls.

I think the hardest people to reach with the good news of Jesus Christ are the "good" people. Those people who try hard to be law abiding, loving and caring—who are honest and hard working, and do nice things for other people—don't think they need a Savior.

But God says, in Romans 3:23, "We have ALL sinned and fall short of the glory of God." He doesn't say only bad people have fallen short, but EVERYONE, good and bad. All people need saving in order to get into heaven. There's no such thing as "good enough." How can it be measured? Where is the cut-off line? How many good things would we have to do to undo the bad things? We cannot earn our way into heaven by being good or doing good. God made it much easier than that.

Jesus says, "I am the way, and the truth and the life. No one comes to the Father except through Me" (John 14:6). This means that Jesus is the only way to God. What had I misunderstood all those years about that?

When my daughter, Justine, died from an inoperable, congenital heart defect, at the age of eighteen months, the Shepherd was trying hard to get my attention. He had to resort to more extreme measures to get me to follow Him, because I had not been listening. He snatched my lamb, my beloved child, and I was left devastated and confused. I felt that if there was a God, He had betrayed me. No loving God would allow such a terrible thing to happen. Like the stubborn sheep left behind, back up there in the meadows, I didn't understand. I didn't know how deep and high and wide was His love for me.

I mourned for a long time. It took me seven years after her death for me to finally respond to the Shepherd's voice, calling to me from up ahead. I'm not sure what made me respond this time, after ignoring it all my life. Maybe my resistance was low that day, my guard down, and He caught me in a humble moment. I wasn't fighting Him anymore. So He caught me when the cover of pride had fallen off just long enough for me to hear Him drawing me near, and I gave in and ran to Him.

In that unexpected moment, I gave up control of my life to Him and let Him have His way, instead of me insisting on mine. I realized I knew nothing compared to Him. Instantly, I felt a huge burden lift from me. In that "unveiling" I could see Jesus holding Justine in His strong arms, so carefully and lovingly, and I knew she was in the best of hands. I knew where she was, and I knew I was going there, too, someday. I felt such joy and expectation, because it all finally made sense to me. It's as if He calls us out of ourselves, and only then are we able to see with new eyes, and hear with new ears, what we could not see or hear before.

That day, all my misconceptions, stubbornness, skepticism, human logic, doubt, pride, guilt, and grief crumbled into a heap—all the things that had become a barrier between Jesus Christ and me, and kept God at such a distance.

Psalm 95:8 states, "Today, if you hear His voice, do not harden your hearts." I think of all the times in the past when the name "Jesus" was mentioned, and I immediately felt defensive and convicted at the same time. That was my heart hardening to His voice. The moment my heart and mind opened to Him, I regretted that I hadn't responded years ago. Why did I resist Him for so long?

All those years without Him, I was one of those stubborn, lost sheep, not knowing my purpose or my destination. Yet everything that happened in my life up to that point, I now know, happened for this very reason: to lead me to Him.

God sent us His Son, Jesus, not to condemn us, but to save us (John 3:17). By giving us His Son, God has given us the only way to Himself, and eternal life with Him. By accepting Jesus, we are saved. It's that simple.

John 10:4 explains, "When He [Jesus] has brought out all His own, He goes on ahead of them, and His sheep follow Him because they know His voice."

Jesus also says in John 10:27-28, "My sheep listen to my voice; I know them, and they know Me. I give them eternal life, and they shall never perish; no one can snatch them out of my hand."

Now that I recognize Jesus as my Shepherd, I listen for His voice, and I follow Him. Unlike before, I trust in Him to lead me because He knows the way; I don't, no matter how much I'd like to think I do at times. My faith is in Him, not in myself anymore. He brought me "out" (of the world) and goes ahead of me—to a beautiful place I've never seen. My own death will be much sweeter, knowing I will see my daughter again when I "catch up." She's waiting for me up ahead. What a wonderful and precious gift.

If I had chosen to stay behind, back up there in those beautiful, green mountain meadows, thinking that was all there was, I would have died never knowing there was so much more. I would never have known my Heavenly Father, never known His love, and never seen my daughter again. I am so thankful that God never gave up on me. He doesn't give up on any of us.

The path the Shepherd now leads me on isn't always easy. Just because I follow Him doesn't mean my life is going to be without any hitches, or that I've miraculously become a perfect person, incapable of any human weakness or error. I'm still that stubborn sheep once in awhile, resisting exactly what I need. Sometimes I step off the craggy and steep path leading to the peaceful valley, and I have to get my focus back on the Shepherd's voice so that I'm going His way and not my own. I'm far from perfect, but I'm still forgiven, still saved and still His.

I realize now that the world's rewards are here only. They can be touched and tasted right now. What the world offers is immediate, but also temporary. What God offers is far-reaching and eternal. His rewards last forever. I've chosen an eternal future and reward beyond this place. No more limitations.

This path I'm now on may seem too narrow and restrictive, or "politically incorrect" in the eyes of the world. It used to look that way to me, too, when I was resisting the Shepherd. But in Matthew 7:13 we find that "the narrow road…leads to life," and "the broad road…leads to destruction." If there are only two roads, and one leads to death while the other leads to life, I know which one I want to be on.

I don't regret that the Shepherd had to come and take my lamb away from me to make me follow Him. It is the most loving thing He could have done. Yes, sometimes I wish I could have watched her grow up and seen her love and raise a family, but that won't matter when I see her again. It will be as if she was never gone from me. God has something even better in mind. He always does, because He loves me so much.

I believe that "the things that have happened to me have actually happened for the furtherance of the Gospel" (Philippians 1:12). There is a greater purpose God has for my life here as well as for when I am with Him in heaven. He has a special purpose for all His children, an identity we can find only in Him, through His Son, Jesus Christ, my Shepherd.

John 3:16-18 – "For God so loved the world that He gave His one and only Son, that whoever believes in Him shall not perish but have eternal life. For God did not send His Son into the world to condemn the world, but to save the world through Him. Whoever believes in Him is not condemned, but whoever does not believe stands condemned already because he has not believed in the name of God's one and only Son."

*My Shepherd

Oh, Shepherd, my Shepherd
Keep watch over me
Please don't let me stray
Keep me close
When darkness surrounds me
Don't let me lose my way.

Chorus

Call me by name
Let me hear your voice
That I may follow
Only You.

Oh, Shepherd, my Shepherd,
Just lead and I follow
Guide me through every storm
And let me know
That when I can't see You
You're near and I'm safe and warm.

Chorus 2x

Tag

Call me by name
Let me hear Your voice
That I may follow
Only You

*Copyright © 1997
Lyrics by Judi Doxey
Music by Wes Retherford
Recorded by Wes Retherford

Growing Up
In God's Grace

JULI DOKEY

Chapter Four

Holy Spirit

Holy Spirit of God
Living in me,
Gift of the Son
Who made me free.
Quiet indwelling
Moving my soul,
Resplendent whispers
Of truth You bestow.
A gentle sweetness
Or convicting word,
A guiding presence,
God's promise insured.

Ephesians 1:13b-14 – Having believed, you were marked in Him with a seal, the promised Holy Spirit, who is a deposit guaranteeing our inheritance until the redemption of those who are God's possession—to the praise of His glory.

John 14:16-17 – "And I will ask the Father, and He will give you another counselor to be with you forever—the Spirit of Truth. The world cannot accept Him, because it neither sees nor knows Him. But you know Him, for He lives with you and will be in you."

2 Timothy 1:14 – Guard the good deposit that was entrusted to you—guard it with the help of the Holy Spirit who lives in us.

Romans 11:29 – ...for God's gifts and His call are irrevocable.

Anointing

Once you've known
The "Anointing,"
You'll never
Be the same,
For He will teach you
How to live
And walk
In Jesus' name.

Romans 8:9b – If anyone does not have the Spirit of Christ, he does not belong to Christ.

John 14:26 – "But the Counselor, the Holy Spirit, whom the Father will send in My name, will teach you all things and will remind you of everything I have said to you."

1 John 2:20 – But you have an anointing from the Holy One, and all of you know the truth.

1 Corinthians 2:12 – We have not received the spirit of the world but the Spirit who is from God, that we may understand what God has freely given us.

Spiritual Perception

Spiritual truths can only be seen
Through spiritual eyes, you see;
So believers enjoy many wonders
Unbelievers cannot perceive.

1 Corinthians 2:14 – The man without the Spirit does not accept the things that come from the Spirit of God, for they are foolishness to him, and he cannot understand them, for they are spiritually discerned.

1 Corinthians 2:8 – None of the rulers of this age understood it, for if they had, they would not have crucified the Lord of glory.

1 Corinthians 2:9-10a – However, as it is written, "No eye has seen, no ear has heard, no mind has conceived what God has prepared for those who love Him," but God has revealed it to us by His Spirit.

When God Speaks

When God is speaking,
My heart starts to pound.
He's letting me know
I'm on Holy ground.
I can push Him away
And pretend I don't hear,
Which I've done before
Because of pride or fear.
But when I submit
And respond to Him,
He's able to use me;
He fills me within,
With His love and power
And joy so complete,
In His purpose so right,
As two cords meet.

Isaiah 30:21 – Whether you turn to the right or to the left, your ears will hear a voice behind you, saying, "This is the way; walk in it."

Walk the Walk

No matter where our life begins,
Whether born to wealth or strife,
It's our ongoing walk that truly speaks
To the character of our life.

Galatians 5:22 – But the fruit of the Spirit is love, joy, peace, patience, kindness, goodness, faithfulness, gentleness and self-control.

1 Peter 2:20b – But if you suffer for doing good and you endure it, this is commendable before God.

Read: Galatians 6:9-10

A Rudder

You'll find unfinished projects here and there,
From creative moments that lost their flare—
Some joyous moments even turned to despair
When life's circumstances took me off somewhere.

There were problems to solve and loved ones in need
When I was called to pray or to intercede.
So I stopped setting goals of my own to feed,
For I was simply on call, and I had to concede.

My childish dreams of success and fame
Were left at "the crossroads of life" in exchange
For whatever God had in mind to arrange,
And not without struggle, my life He claimed.

God made me both a wife and a mother,
For reasons it's taken years to discover.
Sometimes it's those in the shadows of others
Who aren't the great ships, just simply their rudders.

James 3:4 – Or take ships as an example. Although they are so large and are driven by strong winds, they are steered by a very small rudder wherever the pilot wants to go.

Mark 9:35 – Sitting down, Jesus called the twelve and said, "If anyone wants to be first, he must be the very last, and the servant of all."

Matthew 29:26 – "Not so with you. Instead, whoever wants to become great among you must be your servant, and whoever wants to be first must be your slave—just as the Son of Man did not come to be served, but to serve and to give His life as a ransom for many."

Adversity

It shows us how much we need God,
Though it may seem like He isn't there.
It produces character in us,
Though adversity seems unfair.
No use trying to figure it out,
Blaming someone or asking "why?"
We weren't promised a rose garden
Without thorns in abundant supply.
It reminds us we're simply human,
Heartbeats away from eternity;
And it allows us to show others
God's purpose in all adversity.
How we handle it says a lot.
Do we crumble and fall apart?
Or do we pray and be thankful?
Will we stand in the light or the dark?

Psalm 59:16 – But I will sing of Your strength, in the morning I will sing of Your love, for You are my fortress, my refuge in times of trouble.

1 Peter 2:19 – For it is commendable if a man bears up under the pain of unjust suffering because he is conscious of God.

1 Peter 5:7 – Cast all your anxiety on Him because He cares for you.

Read: Psalm 62:5-8 and 1 Peter 1:6-7

Pruning Me

I'm like a grapevine
Rooted firmly in rich ground.
My main stem reaches outward
On strength newly found.

My energy and leaves fall
As cold weather sets in.
I wait upon my Master
To cut and prune my limbs.

This is the time that pains me
And causes me to cry.
He carves me back to nothing
And leaves me asking "why?"

Then I feel my roots go deeper
As my energy focuses there.
Changes take place inside me,
And I know I must prepare.

For then I feel my new growth
More than the season before.
My new branches reach much higher.
My life has been restored.

And because my Master pruned me,
I now am bearing fruits
Because new life flows through me
From deep within my roots.

John 15:1-2 – "I am the vine, and my Father is the gardener. He cuts off every branch in me that bears no fruit, while every branch that does bear fruit He trims clean so that I will be even more fruitful."

John 15:4 – "Remain in Me, and I will remain in you. No branch can bear fruit by itself; it must remain in the vine. Neither can you bear fruit unless you remain in Me."

Deep Roots

When roots go deep
Where water flows,
Abundant fruit
Each season grows.

Shallow roots
Depend on rains;
When there is drought,
No leaf remains.

Deep in God's truth
Where wisdom thrives,
Forever fed
The soul survives.

Without God's word
When trials come,
There is no well
To draw life from.

Psalm 1:3 – He is like a tree planted by streams of water, which yields its fruit in season and whose leaf does not wither.

Jeremiah 17:7-8 – But blessed is the man who trusts in the Lord, whose confidence is in Him. He will be like a tree planted by the water that sends out its roots by the stream. It does not fear when heat comes; its leaves are always green. It has no worries in a year of drought and never fails to bear fruit.

Quiet Spirit

Lord, where is that quiet spirit
I know I'm supposed to possess?
I've lived in the world for so long,
My ego got too big, I guess.
And trying to become submissive—well,
That's what women's lib puts down!
It's hard to go back and relearn again
And turn my life's purpose around.

But, you know, Lord, You are right:
When I'm quiet and I submit,
You work miracles and wonders
In my life that just don't quit!
So I keep working at it, Lord—
This quiet spirit that feels so right—
And I know I can possess it
Once I push the world from sight.

Ephesians 5:12 – Submit to one another out of reverence for Christ.

John 3:30 – "He must become greater; I must become less."

Philippians 2:14 – Do everything without complaining or arguing.

1 Peter 3:3-4 – Your beauty should not come from outward adornment, such as braided hair and the wearing of gold jewelry and fine clothes. Instead, it should be that of your inner self, the unfading beauty of a gentle and quiet spirit, which is of great worth in God's sight.

Proverbs 31:30 – Charm is deceptive, and beauty fleeting; but a woman who fears the Lord is to be praised.

Sometimes I'm Weak

It's not easy to be a Christian;
It's been the hardest challenge I've known.
Trying to live as God wants me to
Makes me sometimes feel so alone
But only because the world is still here,
And it can use its old influence on me,
And I'm pulled away from God's voice inside
As the world steals me momentarily.
While I'm cut off in these situations,
I'm lost from His wisdom and power.
I'm back on my own and floundering again
As I die like a shriveling flower.

It's times like these when I'm failing God
That I learn from my weaknesses best;
For when I reflect on it later, like now,
I can see that I flunked the test.

2 Corinthians 12:8 – But He said to me, "My grace is sufficient for you, for My power is made perfect in weakness."

Lamentations 3:40 – Let us examine our ways and test them, and let us return to the Lord.

1 Peter 4:12-14 – Dear friends, do not be surprised at the painful trial you are suffering, as though something strange were happening to you. But rejoice that you participate in the sufferings of Christ, so that you may be overjoyed when His glory is revealed. If you are insulted because of the name of Christ, you are blessed, for the Spirit of Glory and of God rests on you.

It's All About Him

I'm not here to be the best,
To win awards or to impress.
I'm not here for fortune or fame,
To get applause or make a name.
I don't want to be out on stage
Or be a legend in my old age.
I don't need to succeed in some huge career.
In short, I wasn't born to be great here.
And I'm not comfortable with winning things
Or with the attention winning brings.

I'm better off behind the scenes,
Maybe helping others see their dreams,
Doing the little things I can,
Staying open to the Father's plan.
I just want to be used by Him
And shine the light of His love within,
Perhaps to plant and water some seeds
Or simply fill another's needs—
To point the way to God above
And show a few His kind of love.

Mark 9:35 – Setting down, Jesus called the twelve and said, "If anyone wants to be first, he must be the very last, and the servant of all."

Matthew 20:26 – "Not so with you. Instead, whoever wants to become great among you must be your servant, and whoever wants to be first must be your slave—just as the Son of Man did not come to be served, but to serve, and to give His life as a ransom for many."

Colossians 3:24b – It is the Lord Christ you are serving.

It's Not About Me

Lord, take my focus off of me,
Off my hurts and indignities,
Off the things that keep me bound
To this world where "Me" resounds.
Take any left-over pride.
Take the self I haven't denied.
Put only selfless thoughts in me.
I call on You in humility.
Bind worldly thoughts that interfere.
Lord, I want nothing holding me here.
In Jesus name, Amen.

Psalm 140:24 – See if there is any offensive way in me, and lead me in the way everlasting.

The Biggest Obstacle—Me!

It's been a rough morning, Lord.
I stand convicted in my heart.
Your word spoke loud and clear to me.
My flesh was torn apart.
Forgive me for my ignorance, Lord,
The "old me" was in the way.
On my knees I'm humbled now,
Broken by this day.
Take my heart and heal it, Lord.
Remove all hardened flesh.
Restore in me a new heart, Lord,
The old is such a mess!
You have Your work cut out for You,
Reshaping this old clay.
I went too long without You, Lord,
That's why it hurts today.

Isaiah 64:8 – Yet, O Lord, You are our Father. We are the clay, You are the Potter, we are all the work of Your hand.

Jeremiah 18:3-4 – So I went down to the potter's house, and I saw him working at the wheel. But the pot he was shaping from the clay was marred in his hands; so the potter formed it into another pot, shaping it as seemed best to him.

Psalm 32:1-2 – Blessed is he whose transgressions are forgiven, whose sins are covered. Blessed is the man whose sin the Lord does not count against him and in whose spirit is no deceit.

In Spite of Me

Jesus,

I just want them to see You,
In spite of me.
They could know You
If they looked past me—
With all my inadequacy.
Their expectations are high,
And I'm so awkward and shy—
Easily intimidated;
My abilities are over-rated.
It's hard to be a light for You
When they expect perfection of me.
I don't live up to their degree
Of what they think a Christian should be.
If they could see my heart.
They'd believe in You right from the start.

I can only pray
That in spite of me,
They'll know You someday.
Amen.

2 Corinthians 12:9b-10 – But He said to me, "My grace is sufficient for you, for My power is made perfect in weakness." Therefore I will boast all the more gladly about my weakness, so that Christ's power may rest on me. That is why, for Christ's sake, I delight in weakness, in insults, in hardships, in difficulties. For when I am weak, then I am strong.

1 John 4:5-6 – They are from the world and therefore speak from the viewpoint of the world, and the world listens to them. We are from God, and whoever knows God listens to us; but whoever is not from God, does not listen to us. This is how we recognize the Spirit of Truth and the spirit of falsehood.

Read: 1 John 3:1-3

My Attorney

My worst accuser is me.
I can stop myself cold,
Arguing and condemning;
It can take a death-grip hold.
It's an old destructive voice
That tries to take me down.
That's when I start praying,
Where my best defense is found.
My attorney is Jesus.
His love for me will win the case.
It's in the courts of heaven
My accuser is disgraced.
No self-condemnation
Can win at my expense.
The accusing voice is silenced,
With Jesus at my defense.

Romans 8:31 – What, then, shall we say in response to this? If God is for us, who can be against us?

Romans 9:20 – But who are you, O man; to talk back to God? Shall what is formed say to Him who formed it, "Why did you make me like this?"

Read: Romans 8:33-34

"Well Done"

I forfeit the approval of God
If I'm seeking recognition from man.
When what I do is for God's eyes only,
My reward will come from God's own hand.
What I give in time, energy and love,
My secret prayers and charitable deeds,
Though overlooked and unseen by others,
Will be seen by God most assuredly.
He'll say, "Well done, good and faithful servant."
That's all the reward I will need in the end.
Any glory from others on earth
Pales to the glory my Father intends.

Matthew 6:2 – "So when you give to the needy, do not announce it with trumpets, as the hypocrites do in the synagogues and on the streets, to be honored by men."

Matthew 6:18b – "...and your Father, who sees what is done in secret, will reward you."

Read: Matthew 6:1-8 and 6:16-18 and 25:21

Slaying Giants

Lord, keep my faith bigger
Than the giant I see
Waiting in ambush,
Eager to devour me.
Lord, keep my faith focused
So I see from Your view
That this giant is puny
In comparison to You.

Mark 14:36 – "Abba, Father," He said, "everything is possible for You. Take this cup from me. Yet not what I will, but what You will."

Psalm 71:18 – Even when I am old and gray, do not forsake me, O God, till I declare your power to the next generation, Your might to all who are to come.

Psalm 18:35 – You give me Your shield of victory, and Your right hand sustains me; You stoop down to make me great.

Psalm 116:8 – For You, O Lord, have delivered my soul from death, my eyes from tears, my feet from stumbling, that I may walk before the Lord in the land of the living.

Psalm 34:4 – I sought the Lord, and He answered me; He delivered me from all my fears.

God's Disobedient Child

Oh stubborn and defiant child,
Look on the child you raise,
And see his disobedience,
The rebellion of his ways.
Then look at Me, my child,
And know My fervent plight.
Yet patient I remain with you
While imparting what is right.

Hebrews 5:2 – He is able to deal gently with those who are ignorant and are going astray, since He Himself is subject to weakness.

Hebrews 10:35 – So do not throw away your confidence; it will be richly rewarded. You need to persevere so that when you have done the will of God, you will receive what He has promised.

Hebrews 4:15 – For we do not have a high priest who is unable to sympathize with our weaknesses, but we have one who has been tempted in every way, just as we are—yet was without sin.

Come What May

Lord, You see the worst in me,
Yet still you believe the best.
Nothing I do surprises You;
In spite of myself, I am blessed.
You say my name is engraved
In the palm of your scarred hand,
And that all Your thoughts of me
Outnumber the grains of sand.
You know me better than I do:
My future failings and past sins,
Every day and deed of my life
And each prayer before it begins.
No rebellion dissuades You.
No doubts will push You away.
Long ago You reached Your verdict,
That You'd love me, come what may.

Isaiah 49:16 – See, I have engraved you on the palms of my hands; your walls are ever before me.

Psalm 103:11 – For as high as the heavens are above the earth, so great is His love for those who fear Him; as far as the east is from the west, so far has He removed our transgressions from us.

1 Corinthians 1:8-9 – He will keep you strong to the end, so that you will be blameless on the day of our Lord Jesus Christ. God, who has called you into fellowship with His Son Jesus Christ our Lord, is faithful.

Not to Be Feared

I couldn't save a wild hawk
That had blown in during the night.
The storm had weakened him badly,
But what he died from was fright.
The hawk didn't know I could save him,
That I wanted to help him survive.
He reacted to me by beating his wings,
So I couldn't keep him alive.
If only this hawk could have trusted me,
But I was huge and frightening to him.
If only I could have become a hawk—
He would have let me take him in.

Years later I saw a lesson in this,
That God had intended for me:
I knew why God had to become a man—
In order to set man free.

John 3:17 – "For God did not send His Son into the world to condemn the world; but to save the world through Him."

John 17:25-26 – Jesus prayed, "Righteous Father, though the world does not know You, I know You and they know that You have sent Me. I have made You known to them, and will continue to make You known in order that the love You have for Me may be in them and that I myself may be in them."

In the Making

Thrown for a loop, turned up-side-down,
When I'm just shaking off the dirt from the ground.
I'm getting back up from life's last blow,
While taking a stretch and breathing in slow,
When I'm caught once again by a fist in the face,
Just when I thought I was back in the race.
I'm humbled by life, brought back to my knees,
Where God reminds me: His will I must seize.
It isn't my plans. It isn't my way.
For He's the potter and I'm just the clay.
He sees me finished, perfect and whole,
A vessel designed for a special role.
So His hands keep working to shape and mold;
Then He sets me in fire 'till I come forth as gold.

Job 23:10 – When He has tried me, I shall come forth as gold.

Proverbs 16:4 – The Lord works out everything for His own ends.

Romans 8:28 – And we know that all things work together for the good of those who love Him, who have been called according to His purpose.

Isaiah 64:8 – Yet, O Lord, You are our Father. We are the clay, You are the potter; we are all the work of Your hands.

Proverbs 19:21 – Many are the plans in a man's heart, but it is the Lord's purpose that prevails.

Good Enough

When she was just a little child, she wanted her daddy's love.
She was such a good little girl, but that was never enough.
Everything she said and did, she'd do to make him smile,
To hear the words, "I love you," or be held for a little while.
But her daddy never did these things; he was a self-absorbed man.
He never noticed her need of him, and his love she wouldn't demand.
Why didn't Daddy love her? Was she not pretty or smart?
She wondered what was wrong with her as he continued to break her heart.

Full grown and smart and beautiful, she married and moved away.
She loved and raised a family, though she never felt okay.
She was loved and praised by many and surrounded with hugs and smiles.
But she never felt deserving, for she was still that unloved child.
So many years she struggled to fill the emptiness inside,
Trying to feel good enough until the day her daddy died.

Her only saving grace through life is that she found God's good love,
A perfect and giving Father, the kind she'd always dreamed of.
She could always talk to Him, for He was faithfully there,
And He would hold her anytime; His love He would declare.
He'd kiss away her pain and tears and help her understand
That her daddy didn't feel good enough, and that's how it all began.

Colossians 3:21 – Fathers, do not embitter your children, or they will become discouraged.

Romans 12:9-10 – (NLT) Don't just pretend that you love others. Really love them. Hate what is wrong. Stand on the side of the good. Love each other with genuine affection, and take delight in honoring each other.

Always There

Father, I never have to question
Whether it's a good time or not,
To talk to You when I need to.
I can reach you on the spot.
I never feel hesitant,
Like You cannot be approached,
That there's something I can't say,
Like some etiquette might be broached.
I don't have to speak perfectly;
There's no script I must follow.
You won't correct my grammar
Or make my words feel hollow.
Status doesn't matter to You,
Or mistakes I made in the past;
You are ready, willing and able
To respond to all I ask.
And that is just as it should be,
As a Father should always be there,
Whenever His child comes to Him
Anytime and anywhere.

2 Corinthians 6:18 – "I will be a Father to you, and you will be my sons and daughters," says the Lord Almighty.

Hebrews 4:16 – Let us then approach the throne of grace with confidence, so that we may receive mercy and find grace to help us in our time of need.

Treading Water

Lord, I'm not good at living here.
This world is a crazy place.
I'm not a fighter and scrapper, Lord.
I can't compete in this big race.
I'm not sure I can do this, Lord.
It doesn't take much to do me in.
Sometimes I feel like I'm sinking, Lord.
I never did learn how to swim.
I'm tired of treading water, Lord,
Pushed under by every wave,
Watching all the strong swimmers
Who seem so confident and brave.
But I'll keep on treading water, Lord,
Until You lift me out of this sea.
When I'm with You, I'll know I've won,
Though so many seem ahead of me.

1 Corinthians 9:24-25 – Do you not know that in a race all the runners run, but only one gets the prize? Run in such a way as to get the prize.

2 Corinthians 4:17 – For our light and momentary troubles are achieving for us an eternal glory that far outweighs them all.

Psalm 63:8 – My soul clings to You; Your right hand upholds me.

A Thorn in the Side

Lord, You've given me a thorn in my side.
I can't get away and I just can't hide.
Just when all is well and things seem fine,
I get pricked again by this thorn of mine.
So many times I've tried to pull it out,
Only to have it take root and sprout.
I've even tried to accept it and let it be,
'Till it makes me wince and I want to be free.
What does one do with a thorn in the side?
I guess, like Job did, I'll let You decide.
I'll try to be patient and wait on You
To do what it is You are trying to do.
But Lord, while I'm waiting, could You ease
The pain in my life it causes me, please?

Job 2:10b – "Shall we accept good from God, and not trouble?"

A Prisoner Set Free

Forgiveness doesn't mean you forget
Or excuse what someone has done.
It doesn't mean you smooth it over;
It releases you so that you have won,
Because a prisoner has been set free;
And you discover it is you,
As you dance to the beat of God's heart
And ride the crest of His love anew.

Colossians 3:13 – Bear with each other and forgive whatever grievances you may have against one another. Forgive as the Lord forgave you.

Revealing the Heart

The best indication of
The condition of the heart
Is the speech from our mouths,
Our words and each remark.
The mouth keeps on revealing
Whether we're foolish or wise
And what we place our trust in
And on whom our focus lies.

Matthew 12:34 – Out of the abundance of the heart the mouth speaks.

Proverbs 15:2 – The tongue of the wise uses knowledge rightly, but the mouth of fools pours forth foolishness.

Out of the Heart

The words from our mouths
Speak volumes of our heart.
Our words affect others.
Do they build or tear apart?
As we bare false witness,
When we gossip and malign,
Our words begin their ruin,
As well as self-define.

Matthew 12:34b – "For out of the overflow of the heart the mouth speaks."

Proverbs 13:3 – He who guards his lips guards his life, but he who speaks rashly will come to ruin.

Read: Galatians 5:22 and James 3:5-6

Trouble-making

Slanderous words
From a deceiving heart
Can ruin another
And tear lives apart,
Causing division
Among family or friends;
Untruthful words
Self-condemn in the end.

Psalm 7:15-16a – He who digs a hole and scoops it out falls into the pit he has made. The trouble he causes recoils on himself.

Psalm 101:7 – No one who practices deceit will dwell in my house; no one who speaks falsely will stand in my presence.

Romans 16:17-18 – I urge you, brothers, to watch out for those who cause divisions and put obstacles in your way that are contrary to the teaching you have learned. Keep away from them. For such people are not serving our Lord Christ, but their own appetites. By smooth talk and flattery they deceive the minds of naive people.

Titus 3:10 – Warn a divisive person once, and then warn him a second time. After that, have nothing to do with him.

Bitter Root

Bitterness is like a root
Taking over underground.
You think it can't be seen,
Though it lifts the earth all around.
Bitterness accumulates,
Getting worse as years go by;
And unless the root is cut off,
Its destruction will not die.
Bitterness remembers all—
That's how you know it's there.
You can't forget what happened;
Details follow you everywhere.
You play them over and over;
They consume your every thought.
You drag them out for others,
And the root spreads where you talk.
Accusations are directed
Towards offenders in the past
(Whether real or imagined),
And the root starts growing fast.

A bitter root must be cut,
So it will spread no more.
Bitterness defiles others
While you are keeping score.
You must not keep or share it.
There's only one thing you can do:
Confess it as the sin it is,
For it's not them — it's you.

Hebrews 12:15 – See to it that no one misses the grace of God and that no bitter root grows up to cause trouble and defile many.

Ephesians 4:31-52 – Get rid of all bitterness, rage and anger, brawling and slander, along with every form of malice. Be kind and compassionate to one another, just as in Christ God forgave you. Be imitators of God, therefore, as dearly loved children and live a life of love, just as Christ loved us and gave himself up for us as a fragrant offering and sacrifice to God.

Read: Romans 12:18-19

Character

There's that ten percent in us
That other people can see,
And the other ninety percent
Is our "character" quality.
It's what's below the surface
That determines who we are
When no one else is looking,
Though God sees from afar.
What's happening today
In all aspects of our life
Takes birth in that ninety percent
That determines wrong from right.

Psalm 106:3 – Blessed are they who maintain justice, who constantly do what is right.

Luke 6:43a – "No good tree bears bad fruit, nor does a bad tree bear good fruit. Each tree is recognized by its own fruit."

Read: John 3:19-21 and Romans 8:8

Lord, Give Me Strength

Touch me, Jesus—
I need You right now.
I need to get through this,
And I don't know how.
Hold me above it all—
Bring angels all around;
Let me hear Your word,
As Your Spirit surrounds.
Your way is good.
The world's way is wrong.
It's hard for me here.
It's hard to stay strong.

John 15:19 – "If you belonged to the world, it would love you as its own. As it is, you do not belong to the world, but I have chosen you out of the world."

1 John 5:4 – "For whosoever is born of God overcomes the world."

2 Corinthians 12:8 – "My grace is sufficient for you, My power is made perfect in weakness."

1 Corinthians 1:25 – For the foolishness of God is wiser than man's wisdom, and the weakness of God is stronger than man's strength.

My Prayer

I love You, Jesus, more than I can say.
May I love You more tomorrow than today.
Your love for me still brings me to my knees.
Just use me, Lord; it's You I long to please.
Protect my house and family here within.
Encircle it with angels 'round its brim.
Keep evil from my door and from my heart.
Please shine Your light to guide me through the dark.

Lord, fill me with Your passion and Your peace,
For Your wisdom and Your power never cease.
You're here each time I call Your name.
Enduringly You always stay the same.
Please calm me every time I am afraid.
Help me forgive each time I feel betrayed.
Lord, You know my thoughts and deepest heart,
Have mercy when this world tears me apart.

I give You all I am and all I do.
Give me the strength I need to follow through.
Help me to do the things You've planned for me.
Make me exactly what I need to be.
So many times I feel I let You down.
I lack the ways and words that are profound.
In this world I'm easily dismayed.
I want Your light in me to be displayed.

Lord, keep me filled with joy in knowing You.
I call upon Your Holy Spirit, too.
The world tries to frame me in its design.
But, it's only by You I am defined.
Sweet Jesus, heal the hurts from my past.
Let nothing here take away from my task.
Help me turn everything around for good.
Thank You, Lord, that You've always understood.

In Your precious name I pray, Amen.

John 16:23 – "I tell you the truth, my Father will give you whatever you ask for in my name. Ask and you will receive, and your joy will be complete."

Upper View

Wrestling with wounded thoughts,
Struggling against tears,
I tire of this battle
When my humanness interferes.
My weaknesses start showing,
And I'm vulnerable to pain.
Hurts steal me easily
As I'm humbled in the strain.
But when I call on You, Lord,
My focus shifts to You,
And slowly I'm lifted high
Into Your "Upper" view.
My perspective changes
As I rise above this place.
My thoughts are strong and free again
At peace in Your embrace.

Psalm 140:23 – Search me, O Lord, and know my heart; test me and know my anxious thoughts.

1 Peter 5:6-7 – Humble yourselves, therefore, under God's mighty hand, that he may lift you up in due time. Cast all your anxiety on Him because He cares for you.

Strength

I can stand stronger
After I've kneeled.
I can have victory
Only when I yield.

1 Corinthians 15:57 – But thanks be to God! He gives us the victory through our Lord Jesus Christ.

Psalm 28:7 – The Lord is my strength and my shield; my heart trusts in Him and I am helped.

A Blessing in Disguise

No matter what is happening now,
What trial may be at your door,
If grief has overshadowed you
And you think you can't take anymore;
Take heart, this too, is part of life,
And there is always a good reason.
You must endure this for a while,
For life is a series of seasons.
Through every challenge, persevere.
At the end you'll be surprised,
As God says, "This too shall pass;"
It's another blessing in disguise.
Giving up is not the answer.
There is something better down the road.
Give up your life to Jesus, instead;
He'll renew your hope as He takes your load.
Yes, God's mercies are new each morning.
Give Him your burdens every day.
He has a good purpose and plan for you,
Though maybe unseen, a good reason to stay.

Psalm 68:19 – Praise be to the Lord, to God our Savior, who daily bears our burdens.

Psalm 139:13 – For You created my inmost being; You knit me together in my mother's womb. 139:16 Your eyes saw my unformed body. All the days ordained for me were written in Your book before one of them came to be.

1 Corinthians 3:16-17 – Don't you know that you yourselves are God's temple and that God's Spirit lives in you? If anyone destroys God's temple, God will destroy him; for God's temple is sacred, and you are that temple.

Compassion's Reward

Compassion means "to suffer with,"
To be moved by the pain of others.
As God comforts us in all our troubles,
We must help our sisters and brothers.
If we take the focus off ourselves
And we reach out from our own pain,
It's the most loving thing we can do,
And there's many a blessing to gain.
Giving ourselves and getting more back—
What a splendid way to go through life!
Healing, fulfillment and a sense of worth
Are huge rewards for just being a light.

Romans 12:10 – Be devoted to one another in brotherly love. Honor one another above yourselves.

Touch

The human touch soothes;
It can comfort and relieve.
Without it, babies die
And the elderly grieve.
Touch can heal a broken heart
And calm a frightened child.
It can even ease the pain
Of illness and hard trials.
Touch shows compassion
And demonstrates care;
It also shows acceptance
And that someone is there.
So touch someone today
And then again tomorrow.
You'll find what you've given
Will heal your own sorrow.

Psalm 34:18 – The Lord is close to the brokenhearted and saves those who are crushed in spirit.

1 John 4:8 – Whoever does not love does not know God, because God is love.

Matthew 14:36 – People brought all their sick to Him and begged Him to let the sick just touch the edge of His cloak, and all who touched Him were healed.

Crossing Paths

There have been people who came along,
Who crossed my path and filled my space,
And though I might not have chosen them,
God brought them into that time and place.
God has His reasons, unknown to us,
For placing people into our lives.
And if we receive them as His gifts,
In each one given, there is a surprise.
We can reject some if we want,
But we might miss what God has in mind.
Whether it's for us or the other one,
Friendships here may be God-designed.

Proverbs 16:4 – The Lord works out everything for His own ends.

Hebrews 13:2 – Be not forgetful to entertain strangers; for thereby some have entertained angels unawares.

Proverbs 19:21 – Many are the plans in a man's heart, but it is the Lord's purpose that prevails.

2 Corinthians 4:18 – So we fix our eyes not on what is seen, but on what is unseen. For what is unseen is eternal.

True Winning

A win in the world
Lasts but a moment,
But a win for God
Will always be!
And this is why
My earthly goals
Are geared to gains
That are heavenly!

Matthew 6:21 – "For where your treasure is, there your heart will be also."

Colossians 3:24 – It is the Lord Christ you are serving.

1 John 2:17 – The world and its desires pass away, but the will of God lives forever.

Mountaintop Highs

I've had mountaintop experiences,
Where I wanted to stay,
But God said, "No,
You need to come away
To the valley below,
To all the people in need.
Go refreshed and filled;
In my service proceed."
So many times we seek
That constant mountain high,
Not wanting to come down again,
And our purpose we deny.
We're not here for one long thrill,
And never-ending bliss.
God has things for us to learn and do,
That on the mountain we would miss.

Psalm 138:8a – The Lord will fulfill His purpose for me....

Your Instrument

Lord, I'm just an ordinary instrument.
But that doesn't matter to You.
For if I put myself in Your hands,
Your beautiful music will come through.

Create in me a concert of praise.
Use me to draw lost souls to You.
Let Your perfect love be my song today.
Cause those who listen to hear what's true.

You are the Master Musician.
Play through me Your wondrous song.
Take me and make me Your music.
Through this instrument may others be drawn.

Psalm 33:2-3 – Praise the Lord with the harp; make music to Him on the ten-stringed lyre. Sing to Him a new song; play skillfully and shout for joy.

Psalm 108:3 – I will praise You, O Lord, among the nations; I will sing of You among the peoples.

Ephesians 5:19-20 – Speak to one another with psalms, hymns, and spiritual songs. Sing and make music in your heart to the Lord, always giving thanks to God the Father for everything, in the name of our Lord Jesus Christ.

*Perfect Father

Verses 1 and 2

You are my joy in sorrow
My healing when I'm lame
You calm me when I'm fearful
And cool each angry flame.
You fill me with forgiveness
And help me do what's right
You lift me when I stumble
And make my burdens light.

Chorus

I want to learn to love like You
In all Your perfect ways
And give back all You've given me
While living out my days.

Verses 3 and 4

If I'm proud, You make me humble
When I'm weak, you make me strong
And if I cause a hurtful tear
You show me where I'm wrong.
If I lose my way You find me
When I rush You slow me down
And when I ask for answers
I find them all around.

My Focus

I see God beyond the trials,
I see Him through all pain,
I see Him past each obstacle,
I see Him over the strain.

He stands with arms wide open,
Steadfast in His love,
Always there reminding me,
It's Him I'm in the light of.

So when I focus just on Him,
And not on what is here,
I'm lifted high and carried up,
As the world just disappears.

1 John 5:4 – For whosoever is born of God overcomes the world.

2 Corinthians 4:18 – So we fix our eyes not on what is seen, but on what is unseen. For what is unseen is eternal.

2 Corinthians 4:8-9 – We are hard pressed on every side, but not crushed; perplexed but not in despair; persecuted, but not abandoned; struck down but not destroyed.

Challenge To Open-Mindedness

Chapter Five

Nothing More

No more will be asked of you
And no less will get you in.
You must believe in Jesus;
It's the only way you win.
Now I'm just a messenger,
So don't get mad at me!
I'm commanded to tell you this;
I'm just offering you the Key.
You can take it or reject it,
But I'm just trying to make it clear,
So you know where you are going
When your life is finished here.
God wants you to understand,
So you won't be misinformed.
The world won't want you to hear this.
God wants you to be forewarned.
There's one doorway into heaven,
And it's open to all who see.
There's nothing more required
To get into eternity.

John 10:9 (NJKV) – "I am the door. If anyone enters by Me, he will be saved, and will go in and out and find pasture."

1 John 5:10-12 – Anyone who believes in the Son of God has this testimony in his heart. Anyone who does not believe God has made Him out to be a liar, because he has not believed the testimony God has given about His Son. And this is the testimony: God has given us eternal life, and this life is in His Son. He who has the Son has life; he who does not have the Son of God does not have life.

Open-Minded?

Now, you say you're open-minded,
So you try new things with ease,
And you read the "How To" books
To keep up on all of these.
You try out new philosophies
That say that you come first.
You accept new things that may be wrong
To fill your endless thirst.
You pride yourself on intellect.
You believe in "thinking free."
You think someone who needs Jesus
Is weak and cannot see.
To you, being politically correct
Seems smarter than being good;
So keeping up with the world,
Is better than doing what you should.
You see, I was this "open" once
To all the worldly ways.
I thought Christians were brainwashed,
That they lived in an ignorant haze.
But then one really awesome day,
God revealed Himself to me.
He opened my closed-up mind
So I could finally see.

I saw clearly how blind I'd been,
How closed-minded to what's true.
I thought I had control of my life,
But I really had no clue.
So my pride flew out the door that day
That kept me above such things.
When Jesus came into my heart
I found I knew the secrets of kings.
So, if you think you are open-minded,
But you haven't accepted Christ,
You've actually closed your mind and heart,
And trust me—it's not worth the price!

Proverbs 3:7 – Do not be wise in your own eyes.

Obadiah 3 – The pride of your heart has deceived you.

Read: Romans 12:2

The Greatest Gift

Dearest friend of mine, so precious to me—
There's a gift I'd like to give you that comes with a guarantee.
Because I love you, and I'll always be your friend,
I pray that you would trust the right motives I intend.

I know how you've struggled. My heart has ached with yours;
Yet, how I fumble with my words that might strike defensive chords.
But you ask what God wants of you. How can your answer come
If you refuse to listen to God's answer when He gives you one?

You say you pray for guidance, yet reject God's written Word.
And until you accept Jesus, His answers will go unheard.
Jesus is God's gift to you, the answer to all you ask.
He's tried to get your attention, calling throughout your past.

God says, "You cannot know Me, until you accept My Son,"
That's what He's tried to tell you while you've been on the run.
Oh, how the Father loves you. He wants you for His own;
But as long as you reject Jesus, your prayers can't reach God's throne.

This isn't about "religion." There's no standard you must meet.
It's a matter of giving in to the One who will make you complete.
You may not like how He does things, this God of whom I speak;
But out of all the truths you've heard, in His truth there's no deceit.

God is the One and only true God, whether anyone likes it or not,
So we cannot re-create Him or fit Him into a human slot.
God won't change or waver; that's why they call Him the "Rock,"
And He sent His Son to save YOU. How hard does He have to knock?

Galatians 4:16 – Have I now become your enemy by telling you the truth?

John 5:23 – "He who does not honor the Son does not honor the Father, who sent Him."

John 14:6-7 – Jesus said, "I am the truth, the way and the life. No one comes to the Father except through Me. If you really knew Me, you would know my Father also."

1 John 5:45 – For everyone born of God overcomes the world. Who is it that overcomes the world? Only he who believes that Jesus is the Son of God.

Jesus Saves!

On travels in childhood
At night in the car,
I'd stare out the window
And wish upon a star.
In daylight, vast highways
Stretched out ahead,
And sometimes big boulders
Would stare back that said:

Jesus Saves!

I wondered why anyone
Would write those two words—
A religious fanatic?
It seemed so absurd.
Two meaningless words,
Which all of us could see,
Offended our souls
And wrote on our memories:

Jesus Saves!

Looking back now
To those words upon rocks,
I hear Jesus calling—
My heart hears His knocks.
I know now it's true
Because He saved me.
Look upon the real Rock,
And you, too, will see:

Jesus Saves!

Psalm 19:14 – The Lord is my Rock and my Redeemer.

Revelation 3:20 – "Here I am! I stand at the door and knock. If anyone hears my voice and opens the door, I will go in and eat with him, and he with Me."

Rated "R"

To any unbeliever
I know Jesus is offensive —
Rated "R" for Religion,
So it makes you defensive.
A generic god is all right,
As long as it is not defined.
But "Jesus" is too specific,
When all is relative in your mind.
God in the flesh is too tangible,
His Word too pure and true,
His death for you too personal,
So that makes the subject taboo.

Hebrews 3:12 – See to it, brothers, that none of you has a sinful, unbelieving heart that turns away from the living God.

2 Corinthians 4:4 – The god of this age [Satan] has blinded the minds of unbelievers, so that they cannot see the light of the gospel of the glory of Christ, who is the image of God.

Read: 2 Peter 1:16-18, Hebrews 4:12-13

What Sin?

They are such good people,
Yet still they are lost.
They give from kind hearts,
But what will it cost?
Heaven won't be theirs.
They still can't see Your face.
For all their goodness,
It can't earn Your grace.
Salvation escapes them.
They simply won't give in.
They just can't accept
That Jesus died for their sin.
"What sin?" they keep asking.
"Such good people are we!"
Their separation from You
Is the sin they can't see.

John 3:3 – In reply Jesus declared, "I tell you the truth, no one can see the kingdom of God unless he is born-again."

Ephesians 2:8-9 – For it is by grace you have been saved, through faith—and this not from yourselves, it is a gift of God—not by works so that no one can boast.

Isaiah 59:2 – But your iniquities have separated you from your God; your sins have hidden His face from you, so that He will not hear.

Ecclesiastes 7:20 – There is not a righteous man on earth who does what is right and never sins.

Sin Makes Us Stupid

So flawed are we humans
So vulnerable to temptation
With such foolishness of mind
And with no hesitation
Without even trying
We'll find a justification
Some rationalization
Claiming "victimization"
For the course of action we take
To avoid implication
Due to self-gratification
Or some warped inclination
To save our reputation
Out of desperation
And with great indignation
For self-preservation
To cover-up or whitewash
Our moral degradation
And prevent our own
Character assassination
And humiliation
Because sin makes us stupid!

No rationalization
Can ever dignify
Absolve or cancel out
Our witless deviation.
Our only vindication
And complete exoneration
Is to confess our sin to God
To see it as the sin it is
And accept His Salvation
A right destination
Strength in temptation
Total restoration
A new identification
And renewal of life.

Hebrews 12:1 – ...let us throw off everything that hinders, and the sin that so easily entangles, and let us run with perseverance the race marked out for us.

Read: Romans 7:7-25 (about struggling with sin)

Pride

Pride is a protective shield,
Born out of self-disdain.
It takes its place within someone
Who fears humility's pain.
Pride stands to keep all threat away,
But grows so huge it blinds from sight
The very things that need to be seen.
It can overshadow what is right.
Pride can harden any heart
And freeze the will in man to grow.
What helped to shield a heart from hurt,
Now blocks the way it needs to go.

Proverbs 16:18 – Pride goes before a fall, a haughty spirit before destruction.

James 4:6b – "God opposes the proud but gives grace to the humble."

Unbelief

Boxed in by unbelief
A narrowness of vision
Seeing only this small world
Locked inside its prison.

Squeezed into a worldly view
Unable to see past here
There is no hope beyond
No purpose that is clear.

There's only this brief lifetime
No eternal place to dwell
An unbelieving existence
Leaves nothing left but hell.

Mark 5:36b – "Don't be afraid; just believe."

John 3:3 – In reply Jesus declared, "I tell you the truth, no one can see the kingdom of God unless he is born again."

Rejecting Freedom

He struggles with awful demons
But his weakness just gives in
The darkness then consumes him
And blinds him to his sin.

Freedom is knocking at his door
As he hides away in fear
Holding on to his addictions
Though salvation is so near.

Living such a tortured life
You'd think he'd want to be free
But he always rejects the offer
Whenever he's shown the "Key."

There is a battle being fought
For the soul of this ravaged man
And so I pray that the Savior wins
Salvation is so close at hand.

John 3:19 – "This is the verdict: Light has come into the world, but men loved darkness instead of light because their deeds were evil."

John 3:20 – "Everyone who does evil hates the light, and will not come into the light for fear that his deeds will be exposed."

John 8:36 – "So if the Son sets you free, you will be free indeed."

A Criminal in Paradise

He absolutely deserved death on a cross.
He did unspeakable things in his life.
But while he hung on his cross next to Jesus,
What he witnessed, he knew wasn't right.

As he watched Jesus, he felt compassion
And realized this was an innocent man.
Within hours he believed in the Savior,
And in his heart a miracle began.

So he asked Jesus to remember him.
Instead, Jesus promised him paradise—
And that's where this criminal is today,
With others saved by God's Sacrifice.

The criminal's life was full of mistakes;
He didn't earn salvation with good deeds.
That's why this serves as the perfect example
Of how God simply saves those whose hearts concede.

So if you still think you earn your way to heaven,
That the good you do makes you worthy on earth,
Remember: Jesus showed us that day on the cross
That saving us has nothing to do with our worth.

Luke 23:39-43 – One of the criminals who hung there hurled insults at Him: "Aren't You the Christ? Save yourself and us!" But the other criminal rebuked him. "Don't you fear God," he said, "since you are under the same sentence? We are punished justly, for we are getting what we deserve. But this man has done nothing wrong." Then he said, "Jesus, remember me when you come into your kingdom." Jesus answered him, "I tell you the truth, today you will be with me in paradise."

Romans 10:13 – "Everyone who calls on the name of the Lord will be saved."

The Tough Guy

He's got the best act going—
So authentic he seems,
A man ungoverned;
On no one he leans.
Sturdy and self-willed,
Unrefined and bold,
He will not fit
Into anyone's mold.
Unyielding, resistant,
Set in his ways,
Some men may envy
The way he behaves.
Unattached and untamed,
In charge of his life,
Not wanting or needing
To be known by a wife.
This man who has an answer
For everything that's said
Has only worldly wisdom,
For by the world he's fed.

Could this tough guy
Be tender inside?
Does he feel a huge void
Beneath his false pride?
Could it be he is lonely
And really needs someone
To accept him unmasked
With his strength undone?
If only he could know
The One who knows him,
Who knows his true heart
Behind that stubborn grin.

1 Corinthians 3:18 – Do not deceive yourselves. If any one of you thinks he is wise by the standards of this age, he should become a "fool" so that he may become wise.

Proverbs 11:7 – When a wicked man dies, his hope perishes; all he expected from his power comes to nothing.

Last Night

You didn't know you would die last night
Upon waking yesterday morning.
But by the dusk your life was done—
Suddenly, without any warning.
You lived the day like all other days,
Unaware that you were out of time;
And all of us who heard of your death
Were shocked because you were in your prime.

Several times throughout your life,
The subject of Jesus was mentioned
By friends and close colleagues of yours—
Christians who were well intentioned.
You jokingly laughed at your friends' beliefs,
As you tried to discourage their hope;
But you didn't think you needed Jesus.
To you it was all brimstone and smoke.
Your "good life" was set up exactly
The way you had wanted it to be.
And Jesus didn't fit in the picture,
So you rejected eternity.

Your life was all here and no place else,
With no thought to what lay beyond.
Your hope was in this world you lived,
With no idea that you'd been conned.

Your life ended not knowing Jesus
(God's Son who gives us eternal life).
You rejected God's Key to heaven,
And you could have used it last night.

John 3:3, 7 – In reply Jesus declared, "I tell you the truth, no one can see the kingdom of God unless he is born again.... You should not be surprised at my saying, 'You must be born again.'"

Luke 9:25 – "What good is it for a man to gain the whole world, and yet lose or forfeit his very self?"

Read: Matthew 10:32-33, Mark 16:15-16, Luke 12:8-9, 1 John 2:23

Hypocrites!

You see some pretenders and hypocrites
Perhaps leading double lives and keeping secrets,
While churchly duties they are performing,
And praying in their pews on Sunday morning.
They try to stay awake through the sermon,
But the Pastor might as well be speaking German.
What he says seems irrelevant to their life.
They feel disconnected from that so-called "Light."
They've heard the same scriptures time and time again
Yet still feel unheard at their prayer's end.
They think being Christian means acting "good,"
Not realizing how they've misunderstood.
Just going to church and going through the motions,
Quoting the Bible and doing some devotions,
Doesn't make them a Christian who is saved
If the Book of Life doesn't have their name engraved.
No. Appearing "religious" and "spiritual,"
Or following traditions and rituals,
Won't get them into heaven when they die,
But they seem to think that is their alibi.
They just aren't yet able to comprehend,
Until they take the hand that Jesus extends.
Until they give their hearts and lives to "Him,"
God's Holy Spirit can't even move in
To take up residence inside their heart,
Or remove barriers that keep them apart
From the love of God and all His blessings
And forgiveness for the sins they keep confessing.

They haven't listened to Jesus calling them.
They keep dismissing Him again and again.
Are you one of those hypocrites, too?
If you are, this is what you need to do:
Believe that Jesus is the Son God sent,
That on the cross, it was for YOU He went;
And with your mouth confess you know it's true,
So Jesus can come and live in you.

John 5:39-40 – "You diligently study the Scriptures because you think that by them you possess eternal life. These are the Scriptures that testify about me, yet you refuse to come to Me to have life."

Read: Matthew 6:2 and 6:5-15 and Romans 10:8-13

If Only They Knew

I'm being scrutinized,
Examined all the time,
Like I'm expected to be perfect
Or shine, shine, shine!
They're just waiting,
Hoping I'll make a mistake,
Wondering when I'll "get over this,"
For embarrassment's sake.
They use their little clichés
And typical put-downs,
Such as "She's a Bible banger now";
I've heard it passed around.
And yes, it really bothers me
To be the brunt of their jokes,
'Cuz I'm the sold-out Jesus freak;
I'm fair game for their pokes.
But even though it really hurts,
It's them I'm hurting for,
As they refuse to see the truth
Or hear the knocking at their door.

I'd love to see them in heaven, too,
And know them beyond this place,
Where there's no tears or sorrow
And no past can leave its trace.
But for now I pray for them,
Though they make fun of me.
So little time is left for them
To reach out and take the key.

Isaiah 65:1-3 – "I revealed myself to those who did not ask for me; I was found by those who did not seek me. To a nation that did not call on my name, I said, 'Here am I, here am I.' All day long I have held out my hands to an obstinate people who walk in ways not good, pursuing their own imaginations—people who continually provoke Me to My very face...."

Matthew 5:11-12 – "Blessed are you when people insult you, persecute you and falsely say all kinds of evil against you because of Me. Rejoice and be glad, because great is your reward in heaven...."

Dividing Differences

There's nothing on the outside
That makes you who you are.
It isn't what you look like
Or your birthplace from afar.
It isn't your life-style choice
Or what you eat or wear,
Or which race you belong to,
Or which cause you declare.
Now don't quote me your salary
Or hold up your degrees.
Stop bragging about your career,
For you are none of these.
Just draw me to your heart,
Not the color of your skin.
Show me your character
And who you are within.
Just let me look into your eyes
And know you in my heart,
So we can see how we're the same
And do not stand apart.
We're alike in many ways;
God wants us all to see
That we are nothing on our own,
That united we must be.
So please, no more barriers,
The labels you hide behind.
It's time to take off all the masks
And see what God designed.

We are not the rich or poor.
We are not the black or white.
We are all imperfect humans,
God's sorrow and delight.
If we could all see each other
As God sees us when we're done,
There'd be no need to go to war,
For we would all have won.
Man creates the differences
That cause such big divides;
And if it destroys us in the end,
It will be because of pride.

Read: 1 Corinthians 1:27-29, 31 and 1 Corinthians 1:19-20

The Heart of God

Jesus crossed all barriers
And social boundaries, too—
Cultural and racial ones,
Unheard of for a Jew.
Theology or gender,
Difference didn't matter;
And when He spoke to outcasts,
Boundaries He would shatter.
He approached everyone,
Whether they were wrong or right.
All He saw was their hearts
And their need for God's light.
He truly loved everyone,
Though He knew the worst in them—
Showing us the heart of God,
As He still does, again and again.

Colossians 3:12-14 – Therefore, as God's chosen people, holy and dearly loved, clothe yourselves with compassion, kindness, humility, gentleness and patience. Bear with each other and forgive whatever grievances you may have against one another. Forgive as the Lord forgave you. And over all these virtues put on love, which binds them all together in perfect unity.

Agapé *

The sun shines on each and every flower,
On everything that grows.
It rests upon each living thing;
Throughout the earth it glows.
It even shines on rubbish heaps,
On all things that decay.
It reflects upon each window pane
And on each child at play.
It lingers on the good and bad
And on the strong and weak.
It settles in the old man's beard
And on the baby's cheek.
It lends its warmth to summer days
And in between each storm.
It's there when someone's dying.
It is there when we are born.
The sun shines on each of us;
It doesn't pick and choose.
It shines because that's what it does.
That's all it knows to do.

And this is how our God loves us;
He shines from up above.
His love is unconditional,
It's called "agapé" (love).

*Agapé (Greek): Sacrificial love; God's unconditional love—when one gives his life for those he loves, as Jesus did.

1 John 4:19 – We love because He first loved us.

Revelation 1:16 – His face was like the sun shining in all its brilliance.

Hebrews 4:13 – Nothing in all creation is hidden from God's sight.

Blaming God

They can take God off our money.
They can tear the crosses down,
And seize God's Ten Commandments
From every building in town.
They can remove Jesus from Christmas,
And pervert God's truth and word.
They can eliminate virtue,
So that right and wrong are blurred.
They can laugh at God's warnings,
And refuse to heed His call —
Then watch their world destroy itself,
While they blame God for it all.

Jeremiah 7:19 – "But am I the One they are provoking?" declares the Lord. "Are they not rather harming themselves, to their own shame?"

Jeremiah 8:9b – Since they have rejected the word of the Lord, what kind of wisdom do they have?

Proverbs 21:30 – There is no wisdom, no insight, no plan that can succeed against God.

Philippians 4:18 – For as I have often told you before and now say again, even with tears, many live as enemies of the cross of Christ.

Read: Jeremiah 6:10, 2 Timothy 4:3-4, John 7:7 and 15:23

Baited

How empty life is
When we turn our backs on Him
And toward the new ages,
To follow worldly whims.
When fellowship is severed
And we trust the world instead,
It doesn't take long
Before our joy is dead.
Our spirit grows shallow
When the soul becomes blind.
We follow the deceivers,
With their subtle lies designed
To separate us from God's voice,
To cut us off from His power.
We're easy bait on any hook,
Waiting to be devoured.

Jeremiah 5:23 – But these people have stubborn and rebellious hearts; they have turned aside and gone astray.

1 Peter 5:8-9 – Be self controlled and alert. Your enemy the devil prowls around like a roaring lion looking for someone to devour. Resist him, standing firm in the faith, because you know that your brothers throughout the world are undergoing the same kind of suffering.

Religious Lies

He was turned off by religion,
This stranger I met one day.
He saw my bumper sticker
And challenged me right away.
Oh, how this man frightened me,
So bitter and full of his past,
But I really couldn't blame him;
Too much "religion" he had amassed.
His history was harsh and cruel,
A real "fear of God" beaten in.
Now what's left is a blind man;
"I'm an Atheist," he said with a grin.
All I could do was listen to him;
He wasn't ready to hear
That he'd been a victim of ignorance
By those who crammed him with fear.

So much harm is done in the name of God,
That sadly gives God a bad name.
Too many false religious doctrines
That misinterpret, oppress and shame.
If this man could only see the real truth,
Instead of apparent lies he'd been fed,
He'd see that God didn't hurt him at all —
Just people, who themselves were misled.

2 Peter 3:16 – His letters contain some things that are hard to understand, which ignorant and unstable people distort, as they do other scriptures, to their own destruction.

Ephesians 4:18 – They are darkened in their understanding and separated from the life of God because of the ignorance that is in them due to the hardening of their hearts.

Proverbs 19:3 – A man's own folly ruins his life, yet his heart rages against the Lord.

Projecting

True wisdom sees from all sides,
For there is more than one view.
Yet I'm always amazed
By what some think is true.
They're so sure of themselves
And what they think they see,
Though there's a perspective
They've missed entirely.
If they would stand in the shoes
On the opposite side,
For another angle,
And let go of some pride,
They might be able to see
In a new unbiased way,
That there's a different dimension
To the picture on display.

Everything looks different
From another point of view;
That's why God knows all.
There's His perspective too!
So don't be too quick to judge
From the one angle you see,
Or you will only see yourself
Projected foolishly.

Matthew 7:3-4 – "Why do you look at the speck of sawdust in your brother's eye and pay no attention to the plank in your own eye? How can you say to your brother, 'Let me take the speck out of your eye,' when all the time there is a plank in your own eye?"

John 8:7 – When they kept questioning Him, He straightened up and said to them, "If any one of you is without sin, let him be the first to throw a stone at her."

2 Corinthians 4:18 – So we fix our eyes not on what is seen, but on what is unseen. For what is seen is temporary, but what is unseen is eternal.

The Bible

God's Word is for
Our protection,
Correction
And direction,
At every intersection
Of life,
And the powerful connection
To Him.

Hebrews 4:12-13 – The word of God is living and active. Sharper than any double-edged sword, it penetrates even the dividing soul and spirit, joints and marrow; it judges the thoughts and attitudes of the heart. Nothing in all creation is hidden from God's sight. Everything is uncovered and laid bare before the eyes of Him to whom we must give account.

John 8:51 – "I tell you the truth, if a man keeps my word, he will never see death."

Psalm 119:105 – Thy word is a lamp unto my feet, and a light unto my path.

2 Timothy 3:16 – All scripture is God-breathed and is useful for teaching, rebuking, correcting and training in righteousness, so that the man of God may be thoroughly equipped for every good work.

A Savior Named Jesus

Listen to these words you read.
I promise they are true.
There is a Savior named Jesus,
Who lived and died and rose for you.
His Father lives in heaven
And created you and me.
He sent His Son, named Jesus,
So we could all be free.
We cannot know the Father
Unless we accept His Son.
There's no other way to heaven,
No other way—not one.

Acts 4:12 – Salvation is found in no one else, for there is no other name under heaven given to men by which we must be saved.

John 3:17-18 – "For God did not send His Son into the world to condemn the world, but to save the world through Him. Whoever believes in Him is not condemned, but whoever does not believe stands condemned already because he has not believed in the name of God's one and only Son.

John 5:22 – Moreover, the Father judges no one, but has entrusted all judgment to the Son, that all may honor the Son just as they honor the Father. He who does not honor the Son, does not honor the Father who sent Him.

Your Free Gift Is Waiting

God loves you
Exactly where you are,
Whether you're on Wall Street
Or at the local bar.
He has a gift for you,
And waits 'till you accept.
It's yours just for the taking;
You need not pay to get.
The price was paid already
On a cross at Calvary.
Jesus is God's gift to you.
He died so you could be free.

John 1:29 – The next day John saw Jesus coming toward him and said, "Look, the Lamb of God, who takes away the sin of the world!"

Mark 10:45 – "For even the Son of man did not come to be served, but to serve, and to give His life as a ransom for many."

2 Corinthians 9:15 – Thanks be to God for His indescribable gift!

Lift the Veil

There is someone who is reading
These words that speak out loud,
Who does resist an urge within
To lift the worldly shroud—
A veil that masks the truth enough
To cloud these words you read,
And dims the light upon your heart
Where God now sows His seed.

2 Corinthians 3:14-16 – But their minds were made dull, for to this day the same veil remains when the old covenant is read. It has not been removed, because only in Christ is it taken away. Even to this day when Moses is read, a veil covers their hearts. But whenever anyone turns to the Lord, the veil is taken away.

2 Corinthians 4:3-4 – And even if our gospel is veiled, it is veiled to those who are perishing. The god of this age [Satan] has blinded the minds of unbelievers, so they cannot see the light of the gospel of the glory of Christ, who is the image of God.

Already in Office

God is not a candidate
Who will sell His soul to win.
He's already in office;
Our future is up to Him.
If we like His plan or not
(The Book of Life He wrote),
He still has the final say;
We do not get to vote.
If we disagree with God,
It's because we are wrong.
No getting around it—
He's been right all along!

Isaiah 29:16b – Shall what is formed say to what has formed it, "He did not make me?" Can the pot say to the Potter, "He knows nothing!"

Isaiah 55:9 – "As the heavens are higher than the earth, so are my ways higher than your ways and my thoughts than your thoughts."

Isaiah 45:19b – "I, the Lord, speak the truth; I declare what is right."

My Family-
God's Family

Chapter Six

We Are The Branches

Growing in all directions,
Yet coming from one source,
Some are smooth and stately
While others are gnarled and coarse.
There are those entwined with others
And those entangled or trapped.
Some are hard and unbreakable
While others have bent or snapped.
There are the new and the aged ones
And those just hanging down.
A few are reaching heavenward
As many are twisting around.
Some are hidden among the others
While some are bared and bold.
Some are weight upon another
As from beneath some lift and hold.
Some are bulky and some are fine.
Some are fragile or strong,
Yet every branch upon this oak
Is an instrument in its song.

Psalm 133:1 – How good and pleasant it is when brothers live together in unity.

John 15:5 – "I am the vine; you are the branches. If a man remains in me and I in him, he will bear much fruit; apart from me you can do nothing."

God Put Us Together

I thank God for the love He's given you and me,
To share between each other for all the world to see.
I thank Him for the experiences we've had
And the good that has come from the depths of the bad.
I thank Him for the pleasures as well as the pain,
For the two work together like the sun and the rain.
He has brought us such joy along with the sorrow
And given us hope for the journey tomorrow.
I thank Him for reaching our hearts with His touch
And delivering us from the world and its clutch.
The way hasn't been easy on our mountainous climb,
But His ultimate reward is our gift for all time.

John 15:19 – "If you belonged to the world, it would love you as its own. As it is, you do not belong to the world, but I have chosen you out of the world."

Acts 16:34b – ...he was filled with joy because he had come to believe in God...he and his whole family.

Romans 8:28 – And we know that in all things God works for the good of those who love Him, who have been called according to His purpose.

The Rock Foundation Stands

How bold and courageous we were at first,
When we started our new life together.
We were eager to make the world our home,
Come sunshine or stormy weather.
And, oh, how beautiful the sunshine was then,
Those days filled with endless pleasures.
We sought the "good life" wherever we could,
Accumulating our worldly treasures.

Then storms began brewing in parts of our life
That tested our unity and vigor.
The strength and duration of each one that came
Seemed unyielding, consuming, and bigger.
When each storm ended, we'd begin again,
Finding pieces of our life scattered around.
Our foundation was rebuilt again and again;
Then new storms would shake it back down.

We longed to see the sunshine again
And find the lost pieces of our life.
Then we built our lives upon the Rock,
And a calm came that covered our strife.
Now our days are full of sunshine again,
But the source is a different "Son."
And His solid foundation beneath us
Upholds us with everything we've won.

Matthew 7:24-27 – "Therefore, everyone who hears these words of mine and puts them into practice is like a wise man who built his house on the rock. The rain came down, the streams rose, and the winds blew against the house; yet it did not fall, because it had its foundation on the rock. But everyone who hears these words of mine and does not put them into practice is like a foolish man who built his house on sand. The rain came down, the streams rose, and the winds blew and beat against that house, and it fell with a great crash.

164

Working It Out

I treasure our meaningful talks
'Till near dawn,
Though sometimes tears may flow,
From yawn to yawn.
But clearly we conquer
What started out slow,
Until what remains
Is the good love we know.
Though tired but seeing
A new day ahead,
Enlightened and closer,
We fall into bed.

Job 11:6 – True wisdom has two sides.

Ephesians 4:26 – In your anger, do not sin. Do not let the sun go down while you are still angry, and do not give the devil a foothold.

Psalm 126:5 – They that sow in tears shall reap in joy.

1 Corinthians 13:4-8 – Love is patient, love is kind, it does not envy, it does not boast, it is not proud. It is not rude, it is not self-seeking, it is not easily angered, It keeps no record of wrongs. Love does not delight in evil but rejoices with the truth. It always trusts, always hopes, always perseveres. Love never fails.

After the Storm

When stormy clouds part
And the rains move away,
The earth is left cleansed;
It leaves a new day.
Though the scene is littered
With natures debris,
From rocks moved by water
To uprooted trees,
The landscape is reshaped
With what remains strong,
And the sun again shines
On what was there all along.

Romans 8:28 – And we know that in all things God works for the good of those who love Him, who have been called according to His purpose.

Proverbs 17:14 – Starting a quarrel is like breaching a dam; so drop the matter before a dispute breaks out.

Submission

When two cars are merging,
One has to slow down
To let the other through
So they can both make ground.
A crash will take place
And someone will get hurt,
If both are unyielding;
It isn't going to work.
One needs to submit
For both to make gains;
Then everyone wins,
And harmony reigns.

Ephesians 5:21 – Submit to one another out of reverence for Christ.

1 Thessalonians 5:13b – Live in peace with each other.

1 Peter 3:8 – Finally, all of you, live in harmony with one another; be sympathetic, love as brothers, be compassionate and humble.

Our Time Here Now

I just want to say, "Thank You," Lord,
For giving me this man,
Back when we were just sixteen
And much too young to understand
How deep and wide our love could grow,
And what we would endure—
All the laughter and all the tears
That would seal our bond for sure.

It's always been the little things
That mean the most to me—
Just having him to share my life,
To talk about things like eternity;
To hear him beside me in the night;
And to awaken to his touch.
I could never take for granted
This loving gift that You entrust.

How precious is our time here now
As we make the most of each new day;
To know it could be gone tomorrow
Can change each word we have to say.
We both know how grief feels, Lord,
Like trying to fill an empty chair,
So just the warmth of the other
Is a comfort I am constantly aware.

So, for all our glorious conversations,
The times of silliness and delight,
For the moments we've prayed together,
When we were humbled and contrite,
I just want to thank You, Lord,
For my husband and best friend.
I appreciate his faithfulness,
And the love, through him, You extend.

Thank You, Amen.

Song of Songs 8:7a – Many waters cannot quench love; rivers cannot wash it away.

Protected by Angels

God surrounded us with His angels
One foggy and frightening night.
And if they had not been there,
We would never again have seen daylight.
We witnessed how they steered a huge truck
Like nothing we've seen before,
A miraculous intervention
That no one there could ignore.

I know angels go wherever I go.
I pray for their presence every day.
I'm thankful for God's promise to me
That when I ask, He'll send them my way.

Psalm 91:11 – For He will command His angels concerning you to guard you in all your ways.

Psalm 34:7 – The angel of the Lord encamps around those who fear Him, and He delivers them.

Through My Child's Eyes

Changing colors
To fit your mood
Your eyes reflect
What I can't elude.

From gray to hazel
To green to blue
They mirror the world
To me through you.

Matthew 6:22a – The eye is the lamp of the body.

Proverbs 27:19 – As water reflects a face, so a man's heart reflects the man.

Take Joy in It All

Beloved child, you are still so young,
So much to know and you've just begun.
You've started a new life out on your own,
But that doesn't mean you are ever alone.
All that happens and all that life brings
Will give you gifts and teach you things.
As God is my witness to what life holds,
It's all about Faith as it all unfolds.

So don't be afraid of what lies ahead.
Try not to worry or be filled with dread.
Just let life bring whatever it may,
And with joy in your heart, enjoy each day.
When hardships come, as they surely will,
Don't let them steal faith or your spirit kill.
For momentary struggles soon pass by,
Though they may leave you questioning, "Why?"

Look for the good, the gifts in each one,
And do any growing that needs to be done.
God has good reasons for all that takes place,
As He constantly holds you in His embrace.
There is so much to live for that can't be seen,
Known only to God beyond what we can dream.
So live, and enjoy what you have right now.
Be thankful for everything that God allows.

Don't let what may happen take joy away.
Don't let worldly things lead you astray.
Be careful not to add to what's really there,
And when you look at others, don't compare.
Keep your focus on what is good and right,
And all the reasons you have for delight.
When things do go wrong, there's no use in blame,
For there is no growth without some pain.
You have a purpose, though it may not be clear.
Just listen to God and let Him steer.
Remember, God loves you, for you are His child.
The day you were born, all His angels smiled!

Proverbs 3:5-6

All a Mother Can Do

As a teen, you shielded secrets;
You hid your thoughts from me.
But I knew how you struggled;
Though you're grown, I still can see.
Whenever I tried to help you,
You'd always push me away;
And that's when I realized:
All a mother can do is pray.
Once I could lift you when you fell,
I could lead you by the hand.
I could wipe away your every tear;
Then, as now, I could understand.
Just as Mary had to watch from afar,
Helpless to save her Son from pain,
As He struggled bearing His cross,
I feel I am doing the same.
She couldn't change the way it was
Or take His burden away;
And as I watch you struggle now,
All a mother can do is pray.

1 John 5:4-5 – ...for everyone born of God overcomes the world. This is the victory that has overcome the world, even our faith. Who is it that overcomes the world? Only he who believes that Jesus is the Son of God.

1 John 4:4b – ...because the One who is in you is greater than the one who is in the world.

Mark 5:36b – "Don't be afraid; just believe."

Bloom

Just bloom where you are planted,
Right where God wants you to be.
Though you'd rather be someplace else,
If you choose where you are, you'll see:
You can bloom where you are planted;
You can be a magnificent flower
That brings joy to the lives of others.
While here, God gives you that power.

James 3:13 – Who is wise and understanding among you? Let him show it by his good life, by deeds done in the humility that comes from wisdom. 3:17 But the wisdom that come from heaven is first of all pure; then peace-loving, considerate, submissive, full of mercy and good fruit, impartial and sincere.

Read: The Wife of Noble Character – Proverbs 31:10-31

Contentment

If you didn't always want more,
Then you would be content.
You'd be perfectly satisfied,
Thankful for all God has sent.
Be grateful for all you have.
God supplies your every need.
If you take care of all God's given,
You will be rich indeed.

Hebrews 13:5 – Keep your lives free from the love of money and be content with what you have, because God has said, "Never will I leave you; never will I forsake you."

Philippians 4:12 – I know what it is to be in need, and I know what it is to have plenty. I have learned the secret of being content in any and every situation, whether living in plenty or in want.

Passing the Love On

You grew to be so lovely,
And you have a daughter of your own.
How did this happen so fast?
Oh, how these years have flown!

You were a genuine gift of joy,
Created through God's hands for me,
And now He's given you one, too.
That's how He loves us perfectly.

I watch you with your little girl.
Your love so softly spilling out.
My life has come full circle.
It's a miracle; there's no doubt.

You hold her precious hand in yours
And walk with her awhile,
Just as I've walked with you,
In these days so full of smiles.

Take these days and hold them close;
So quickly they will fly.
One day you'll feel what I do now—
God's extraordinary, heart-filling sigh.

Pass the love on... Love, Mom

Postponed

Strong, whole and healthy,
I see you running there,
With Jesus right beside you,
And the wind in your hair.
You're so loved and cherished;
I could ask for no more.
This world can't reach you
Where you now soar.
You were too fragile
To be here, we know,
So what better place
For you to go?
To you it will seem
Like a minute has passed,
When we meet again—
Reunited at last.

But I'm missing you now.
I'm the one who must wait,
While you dance with Jesus
In your perfected state.
Though it does my heart good
To know you are home,
I feel caught in time
In a place called Postponed.

Psalm 34:18 – The Lord is close to the brokenhearted and saves those who are crushed in spirit.

Psalm 90:4 – For a thousand years in your sight are like a day that has just gone by, or like a watch in the night.

Called to Love

I was called to love a child
For his sake, not mine;
And that's the difference between
Selfish love and love divine.
Though love at first was not returned,
I was called to give my heart,
And God then blessed my efforts;
He did the miracle part.
Love can be a sacrifice,
A commitment we must make,
Like the love that Jesus gives,
Not for Him, but for our sake.
His love is unconditional;
It may never be returned,
But He loves us for loving's sake —
A love that is never earned.

Matthew 5:46 – "If you love those who love you, what reward will you get?"

Prayer for "Billy"

Oh, Lord, please save
This little boy for me.
You're the only One
Who can set him free
From a past so twisted
And full of hate.
Please help him forget
Before it's too late.
He needs a new life,
To start over again,
And I pray he'll never
Pass on what happened then.
Lord, help him grow sturdy
And spiritually strong.
Stay beside him and guide him,
All his life long.

Ecclesiastes 3:11 – He has made everything beautiful in its time.

Matthew 18:5 – "And whoever welcomes a little child like this in My name welcomes Me."

Let It Go

Like a snarling dog that won't give up its bone,
He's a raging child throwing stick and stone.
He holds on tight to a hurting past,
While everywhere his anger is cast.
It seeps out here and spills over there.
It causes those around him great despair.
And when he turns the anger on himself,
Depression blocks all joy and health.

If all that pain he holds to so tight
Could be given up into God's light,
He'd find that what he's holding onto
Is all that's left of what he once knew.
His pain keeps him tied to the very ones
Who hurt him most when he was young.
But staying mad is what makes him feel strong,
Though sadness is what's really wrong.

Until he leaves that awful life behind,
It's only by his anger he'll be defined.
If bitterness takes root in his soul,
It will trap his life in its control.
If he could just give God all his pain,
And let it fall away just like the rain,
He'd see his consuming anger disappear,
And he'd let the love around him near.

The past won't ever give him what he missed.
It makes the present unable to exist.
He must give up the fight and let it go.
It's time for him to live a new life and grow.

Ephesians 4:31 – Get rid of all bitterness, rage and anger, brawling and slander, along with every form of malice.

A Miracle in Progress

I hated what I saw in him:
The result of someone else's hate.
What they yanked away from him
Left only damage in its wake.
They took away his trust and hope,
Maiming him with fear and shame.
They stole his dignity and joy.
No innocence in him remained.
Now here he was so tensed and closed.
How could I ever reach his heart?
It looked as if I never would—
So much to undo; where should I start?

So I gave this child up to my God.
For every miracle I prayed.
God would do the impossible.
It was this promise to me He made.

Now stands before me, straight and strong,
That boy who has become a man.
And I can see God's heart in him,
As I am awed by God's good plan.

Psalm 72:12 – For He will deliver the needy who cry out, the afflicted who have no one to help. He will take pity on the weak and the needy and save the needy from death. He will rescue them from oppression and violence, for precious is their blood in His sight.

Granny's Old King James

Granny's old Bible lists some birthdays
Back to eighteen-seventy-eight.
The leather cover is crumbling now,
But on its message I contemplate.
I think back how Granny prayed for me,
That I would someday know God's Word;
And now her prayers have been answered,
Though she died before this occurred.
I remember her rocking and praying.
I'd never seen anything like that—
Singing and praising Jesus out loud,
With this very Bible in her lap.
As I'm reading the words she underlined,
A pressed flower falls from the pages;
It's as if Granny is sending me
A blessing from the Rock of All Ages.

What Granny underlined in her Bible:

St. John 8:51 – "Verily, verily, I say unto you, If a man keep my saying, he shall never see death."

Read: Psalm 23, Psalm 26 and Psalm 119:33-40

Looking Both Ways

I'm passing now between two stages,
Helping my parents as each one ages,
And caught by my grandchild's joyful play.
I see both tomorrow and yesterday.
Both ends of life are tugging at me,
As I see what's to come and what used to be.

Philippians 4:12-13 – I know what it is to be in need, and I know what it is to have plenty. I have learned the secret of being content in any and every situation, whether well fed or hungry, whether living in plenty or in want. I can do everything through Him who gives me strength.

Isaiah 58:11 – The Lord will guide you always; He will satisfy your needs in a sun-scorched land and will strengthen your frame. You will be like a well-watered garden, like a spring whose waters never fail.

Sierra Justine

Your name is like the mountains;
"High view" is what it means,
For you will be a child of God,
Held in His high esteem.
You will see through His eyes.
His vision will live in you.
He'll hold you up above this world
Where you'll see from His high view.

Love, Gramma 2000

Mark 10:16 – And He took the children in His arms, put His hands on them and blessed them.

Skylar Marie

I see a timeless circle,
Layers and layers of life,
A circle that never ends,
Generations come to light.
The blending of families
Here in your tiny face,
The past and the present
Asleep in my embrace.
A precious part of each of us
Continues in you, child,
Never to be forgotten,
A point of reconcile.
This never-ending circle
I celebrate in you
Is God's confirmation;
His presence here is true.

Love, Gramma 2001

Matthew 11:25 – At that time Jesus said, "I praise You, Father, Lord of heaven and earth, because You have hidden these things from the wise and learned, and revealed them to little children."

Alexander Elijah

Welcome to the arms of love,
Not just ours, but God's above.
Born to heal old memories,
Some painful wounds you'll ease.
Just what your daddy needed;
His dreams have been exceeded.
He has a place to put his heart.
You've given him a brand new start
By giving him a family,
Something he never thought could be.

Love, Gramma 2003

Matthew 19:14 – Jesus said, "Let the little children come to Me, and do not hinder them, for the kingdom of heaven belongs to such as these."

Randy William

I never saw your daddy
When he was a baby like you.
He came to me when he was nine,
With no photos I could look to.
But when I held you at your birth,
I saw your daddy in your face;
And in that moment God gave me
What I had missed but now embrace.
You have his eyes and wrinkled brow,
So when I look at you I see
The missing photographs of him
When he also was a baby.
You've given me a part of him,
The piece that was never there.
And now you've given him that. too,
While at his heartstrings you tear.
Now he has the chance to try
To show the love he was once denied.

Love, Gramma 2003

Proverbs 17:6 – Children's children are a crown to the aged, and parents are the pride of their children.

Tigger

A Lesson in Staying in the Arms of God

Psalm 32:7 – You are my hiding place; You shall preserve me from trouble....

I miss my cat, Tigger. She disappeared several years ago, and I can only assume that a coyote got her in one of those moments when she wasn't being watchful. She was probably stretched out on a big, warm bolder somewhere, far from my protection, dozing in the sun, and unaware of any danger lurking nearby.

You may think it a little strange that I would be telling you a story about a cat, and stranger still, that this cat would have anything to do with staying in the arms of God. But, bear with me. Daniel 2:28 says, "There is a God in heaven Who reveals mysteries"—even through a cat.

Tigger was pretty ordinary looking. There was nothing awfully special about this feline, accept how I felt towards her. I've had dozens of cats over the years, usually several at a time. I didn't do anything to acquire her; she just showed up one day, and that was that.

Tigger was a tabbie, more on the brownish side, and had yellow eyes. She did have one orange spot on her back, as though she had tried to be a calico, but never quite succeeded.

When I first saw her, it was clear she was afraid of people. She was skittish and on the defensive. It became a challenge for me to win her over, to get her to trust me like all my other cats did. But this cat didn't think she needed me for anything, though she was sneaking cat food off the back porch when no other cats were around. She stayed off by herself, but I could see her watching me from a distance, following me with those yellow eyes. If I got too close to her, she'd run.

Several months later, I noticed that Tigger hadn't been coming to eat for a few days. That night I heard a cat calling out all through the night, some distance away, as though it was trapped or hurt; it sounded so distressed. I was worried that it was Tigger.

The next day I looked and called for her, but I didn't find her until that evening. She couldn't walk. She must have dragged herself by her front legs all the way home. Her right back leg was almost completely severed, and torn open to the bone. She was dirty and help-less. I wasn't sure I could even touch her, for fear she would fight me. But I was going to try anyway.

I was surprised when she allowed me to just pick her up and carry her into the house, without the slightest struggle. There was no fight left in her. She had nowhere else to turn. But I knew there was no way I could get her into a car and take her to the vet, either. So I laid her on a blanket in the house where I could watch her closely, feed her, care for her, clean her up and doctor her leg. I had doctored many animals before.

I talked soothingly to her, saying, "Nice Tigger. You can trust me." She began responding to my voice with contented purring. That moment when she put herself into my hands, to do with her as I pleased, a real connection took place between the two of us, as compassion filled my heart for her. She began talking to me, too, whenever I was nearby. It was the turning point in our friendship, a friendship that would last nine years, and that would, of all things, teach me more about the two-way relationship I had with God that I was still so new at during that time in my life.

Tigger was completely dependent on me for about two weeks. She let me feed her, clean her and disinfect her wound, and carry her outside to go to the bathroom twice a day. And best of all, she let me comfort and love her. I could hold her in my lap with no resistance from her. She trusted me. She knew she had to. She really needed me after all.

Soon she was hobbling around. The leg had healed, although it was crooked. She was able to put more weight on it with each day.

One day, I lifted her to my face and told her, "Pretty Kitty, it's time to go back out into that world." I put her back outside with the rest of the cats. She was different than before. She seemed humbled and less threatened, so the other cats didn't chase her away anymore. She was part of the family. She still went off by herself sometimes, usually for a few days; but she would always come back looking for me, like she needed a "fill-up."

When I'd see her in the distance, I'd call her name and she would come running. Oh, the many times I bent down to pick her up and hold her tightly in my arms. Then I'd sit with her in my lap and feel the tension leave her body as she relaxed, and was lulled into a purr. Each time we sat together, I would imagine how God would hold me—each time I'd been away from Him for awhile, how He would welcome me back with open arms and then give me His strength to go back out into the world again. I came to appreciate and look forward to those times with Tigger. All my tensions would ease as well. She would always be the one to decide when she'd had enough filling up, then down and off she would go again, seemingly strengthened for the world.

Months later, Tigger disappeared. I looked and called for her for days and days, but she didn't come this time. I had never missed a cat like that before.

About a year later, my husband and I went for a long walk one evening. We went past an old two-story house that was one of the first homes built in our small rural town. A new housing development was being built all around it, and we were walking through the framed skeletons, talking and laughing about something, when I heard a faint "meow" off in the distance, near the old house. My gut told me to listen and look. Then I spotted a cat sitting way far off, looking at me. "Could it be?" I thought. So I called out, "Tigger." The cat looked startled. I called again, "Tigger?" And the cat came bounding towards me, full speed, gimpy leg and all, meowing all the way. And when I saw that one orange spot on her back, I knew it was my Tigger! I was never so happy to see a cat in all my life. I couldn't believe it! I scooped her up in my arms, and she was already purring, so glad to see me. It felt so good to hold her again.

We were stunned. It had been a year since we'd seen her. Where had she been all this time? So many questions would never be answered. If only she could have talked. What a story she could have told, I'm sure.

We turned for home as I held her in my arms. But the closer we got to home, the more she struggled to get away. I managed to hold onto her all the way back, and once we got her into the house, she settled down a bit, probably because I put some food in front of her. She really didn't look any worse for wear. She must have been eating, even though she was hungry. But later she began crying to get out. I didn't want to keep her against her will. After she had been pacing back and forth for some time, I finally let her out. She was gone all night.

The next morning when I opened the front door, I found a tiny baby kitten right there on the door step. It was an exact replica of Tigger, minus the orange spot on its back. It was all alone. I didn't see Tigger anywhere. I sat and held the baby kitten for a long time, wondering and waiting. Had Tigger gone off to get another kitten from somewhere? It was as if she brought me a gift, an offering, something important to her. Tigger finally came back, but without another kitten. She seemed content with just the one. We accepted her kitten and just enjoyed having Tigger home again.

A few years later, we moved to a 320-acre ranch, out in the mountains of the back country. We took all our animals with us, including Tigger. She adjusted well, as did all of us. But we did lose a few cats through the years to coyotes, when they wandered off too far. Tigger would still go off by herself for a few days at a time, and then come home and find me. Sometimes she would bring me a dead squirrel or gopher as a gift and set it at my feet, or leave it on the front door step. She would also follow me on long walks around the ranch, sometimes for miles.

Many times we would sit quietly in a chair together. She still seemed to need that now and then, and so did I. It seemed to be a time of "filling" for her, and then she could go out and face the world again. I looked forward to those times with her. When we sat together, I was always reminded of how God would do the same thing with me, especially if I had been running on "empty" for a while, and I had to come running back to Him to get filled. Holding her made me feel closer to God, just for that reason.

I would go back in my mind to when Tigger first came into my life, and how she stayed away at a distance, not trusting me and thinking she didn't need me, only the food I put out every day. She was just like I once was, keeping my distance from God, not thinking I really needed Him for anything. Then something happened one day that made her realize she did need me. And when she put herself into my hands, she knew she could trust me with her very life. How Tigger's perception of me changed was exactly how my perception of God had changed.

Like Tigger had come to me that day, broken and mangled, I came to God one day. I needed Him, but I was standing back, only observing Him, and relying on myself. I came to Him broken by life's circumstances—circumstances that were completely out of my control—humbled from having used up all my own strength, ready to just give in, with no more fight left in me. And, just like Tigger gave in to me, I also put myself in God's hands, and I gave up the struggle to resist a personal relationship with Him. It was then that God was able to reach down and pick me up, and I didn't resist. Tigger and I had this yielded condition in common.

Tigger was about nine years old when she disappeared for good. I wondered for a long time if she would show up in my life again, like she had done once before. But, no, only in my memory, as a reminder for me many times since then that I need to spend time with God.

Sometimes my focus isn't on God, and I wander off my own way, distracted by life's trials and the lure of the world's ways. In Isaiah 53:6 it says, "We all, like sheep, have gone astray, each of us has turned to his own way." I'll launch off in some direction without the faintest thought as to where God may want me to go, and then wonder why things aren't going too well, or why I'm tired, confused, disappointed, resentful or hurting. But God uses the memory of a cat to remind me that I need to come back into His arms, and His way.

Proverbs 3:5 says, "Trust in the Lord with all your heart and lean not on your own understanding." Too many times I've neglected to go to God first. To lean means "to shift your weight onto." I need to shift towards God, to look towards God, to go back into His arms and give Him my burdens.

I feel secure and at peace in God's arms, just like Tigger did in my arms. It's always such a relief when I let Him have me. So why, after I get filled up with Him, do I jump off His lap and run off again? It's a human thing. But God has His reasons for this and won't force us to stay.

In Psalm 32:7, David says, "You are my hiding place; You preserve me from trouble." God preserves me. That doesn't mean I won't have trouble in my life; trouble is a given. Preserve means, "to keep from harm," "to guard," "to keep from decay," "to maintain and keep for future use." So, as long as I stay focused on Him during my troubles, I will be preserved. I have to be leaning on Him, and depending on Him, and listening to Him. And the bonus is that all my troubles will prepare me for future use! How awesome! That also means that when I've jumped off His lap and wander off, there will be things I'll learn from my experiences that God can use for His glory, and my good.

I couldn't preserve Tigger when she was away from me. I couldn't protect her from harm out there in the world. But God can do that for me. I like the idea that I can stay above the troubles in my life, and that they don't drag me down into despair. That's preservation. God is right there with me, carrying me over it, and teaching me all the way.

So whenever you feel yourself getting caught up in your troubles, and the circumstances and distractions in your life are overwhelming—if you feel on edge, over-reacting, afraid, complaining, in doubt or weak—would you do me a favor? Think about Tigger. And then, go climb up into God's lap, and stay there. He loves to hold you in His strong arms. Everything He is, will sustain you—through everything.

James 4:8 – Come near to God and He will come near to you.

Gentle Giants

Soft silhouettes in the morning mist,
Majestic oaks stand as if to resist
The worldly bombardments that living brings,
A vision of strength among human things.
Two gentle giants, like sentries on guard,
With arms reaching over my front yard.
Always there like good friends should be,
They shadow my life so graciously,
Framing the beauty I see every day.
Sometimes their presence moves me to pray.

Psalm 18:19 – He brought me out into a spacious place; He rescued me because He delighted in me.

The Final Humbling

Growing old is looming ahead.
It's guaranteed if you're not dead.
Try as you may to slow it down;
Its purpose in life is profound.
Aging is the last humbling phase,
Submitting to your ending days.
It's letting go of youth and health,
Of home and friends and perhaps wealth.
You lose these things along life's road,
As mind and body both erode.
All the things you take for granted,
Though once yours are soon recanted.
This, too, is part of God's good plan,
The final humbling of each man,
'Till there is nothing left but "Him"
In every heart that lets God in.
On God alone can you depend
When all you have comes to an end.
This can be done with thankful praise,
With joy and hope that can amaze!

Romans 12:12 – Be joyful in hope, patient in affliction, faithful in prayer.

1 Corinthians 13:12 – Now we see but a poor reflection as in a mirror; then we shall see face to face. Now I know in part; then I shall know fully, even as I am fully known.

John 6:40 – Jesus said, "For my Father's will is that everyone who looks to the Son and believes in Him shall have eternal life, And I will raise him up at the last day."

2 Corinthians 4:16 – Therefore we do not lose heart. Though outwardly we are wasting away, yet inwardly we are being renewed day by day.

Psalm 92:14 – They will still bear fruit in old age, they will stay fresh and green.

Beginning at the End

I have nothing to dread
At the end of my life.
Each day that passes
Brings God closer in my sight.
Each morning I rise,
I am nearer the day
When I'm held in His arms
As He lifts me away.
I have this future hope
That reaches beyond here,
Where my real home is,
With each day I draw near.
What is there to lose
If my life is in Him?
When I'm finished here,
My real life will begin.

Psalm 73:26 – My flesh and my heart may fail, but God is the strength of my heart and my portion forever.

Jude 8:20-21 – But you, dear friends, build yourselves up in the holy faith and pray in the Holy Spirit. Keep yourselves in God's love as you wait for the mercy of our Lord Jesus Christ to bring you to eternal life.

A God Moment

God comes near...
I feel Him here,
Intersecting time...
His with mine.
The moment changes.
Light rearranges.
Golden warmth surrounds.
Such love astounds.
His peace so still...
My heart does fill.
The world disappears,
With all my fears.
I'm held in a psalm,
Soothed in His calm.
Filtered and pure,
His presence secure.
Hope is complete...
Assurance sweet.

Psalm 145:18 – The Lord is near to all who call on Him, who call on Him in truth.

1 Corinthians 13:10 – But when perfection comes, the imperfect disappears.

God's Love

His love is a place
Of safety and rest,
Where trust is constant,
Proven and blessed.
It's a place to linger,
A well to draw from;
It's wide open arms
Into which I can run.
His love is a place
To store up the heart—
My sanctuary,
My home and hearth.

Psalm 23:1-3 – The Lord is my shepherd, I shall not want. He makes me lie down in green pastures, He leads me beside quiet waters, He restores my soul. 23:6 Surely goodness and love will follow me all the days of my life.

Letting Go......
Letting God

Chapter Seven

Let Go and Let God

Don't stop at the mystery.
Don't ask why.
Don't wonder or question;
Just trust God on high.
Just pass on through
And let Him lead.
Go where He takes you
And be blessed, indeed.

Proverbs 3:5 – Trust in the Lord with all your heart and lean not on your own understanding.

Romans 12:2 – Do not conform any longer to the pattern of this world, but be transformed by the renewing of your mind.

Proverbs 19:21 – Many are the plans in a man's heart, but it is the Lord's purpose that prevails.

The Safest Place

The safest shelter
In this uncertain place
Is right in the center
Of God's will and grace.

Psalm 32:7 – You are my hiding place; You will protect me from trouble and surround me with songs of deliverance.

Psalm 57:1b – I will take refuge in the shadow of your wings until the disaster has passed.

Psalm 63:8 – My soul clings to You; Your right hand upholds me.

Psalm 118:8 – It is better to take refuge in the Lord than to trust in man.

"Tetelestai!"*

Just before He died upon the cross,
Before man knew what God's love would cost,
Jesus cried out with one last sigh,
As it was finished, "Tetelestai!"
All the prophesies had been fulfilled,
Though it may seem that truth was killed.
His death paid for all the sins of man,
And it was part of God's greatest plan.
He accomplished His purpose on earth,
Redeeming those who know His true worth.
The blood of Jesus was shed for us all,
Prophesy fulfilled in His last call.

* (Greek) meaning, paid in full; it is finished, done. Jesus had fulfilled all the prophesies of the Old Testament by His death on the cross. His sacrifice was the only solution to the problem of sin and death for man.

1 Corinthians 1:18 – For the message of the cross is foolishness to those who are perishing, but to us who are being saved it is the power of God.

1 Peter 2:24 – He Himself bore our sins in His holy body on the tree, so that we might die to sins and live for righteousness; by His wounds you have been healed.

Philippians 2:6-11 – ...Christ Jesus, Who, being in very nature God, did not consider equality with God something to be grasped, but made Himself nothing, taking the very nature of a servant, being made in human likeness. And being found in appearance as a man, He humbled Himself and became obedient to death, even death on a cross! Therefore God exalted Him to the highest place and gave Him the name that is above every name, that at the name of Jesus every knee should bow, in heaven and under the earth, and every tongue confess that Jesus Christ is Lord, to the glory of God the Father.

*What Kind Of Love Is This? (a hymn)

Verse 1 and 2

What kind of love is this that knows no bounds,
That leads and protects, heals and astounds?
And who am I? Who am I, to be loved like this,
To know this kind of love?
What kind of love is this that never fails,
That went to the cross to be pierced with nails?
And who am I? Who am I to be loved like this,
To know this kind of love?

Chorus
He loved me so...enough to die.
Why would He do this for me?
He loved me so...now I know why.
He died for me to set me free,
Forgiving me...He set me free.

Verse 3 and 4

What kind of love is this that shows the way,
That leads us back home whenever we stray?
And who am I? Who am I to be loved like this,
To know this kind of love?
What kind of love is this that takes our wrongs,
That fills the heart it saves with joyous songs?
And who am I? Who am I to be loved like this,
To know this kind of love?

* Copyright © 1995
Lyrics by Judi Doxey
Music by Terese Lekas (Richardson)

Tell the World

The good news of Jesus is the truth.
That's why He commands us to teach it.
We have no right to keep it to ourselves.
It is for the world, and we must reach it.

Mark 16:15 – He said to them, "Go into the world and preach the good news to all creation."

Romans 10:15 – …As it is written, "How beautiful are the feet of those who bring good news."

Romans 10:14 – How, then, can they call on the One they have not believed in? And how can they believe in the One of Whom they have not heard? And how can they hear without someone preaching to them?

2 Corinthians 2:14-16 – But thanks be to God who always leads us in triumphal procession in Christ and through us spreads everywhere the fragrance of the knowledge of Him. For we are to God the aroma of Christ among those who are being saved and those who are perishing. To the one, we are the smell of death; to the other, the fragrance of life. And who is equal to such a task?

We Need More Lights

God's light is being obscured everywhere,
While darkness overshadows the world unawares.
In this darkening world, we need more lights
To shine, shine, shine with all of their mights!

Matthew 5:14-16 – "You are the light of the world. A city on a hill cannot be hidden. Neither do people light a lamp and put it under a bowl. Instead they put it on its stand, and it gives light to everyone in the house. In the same way, let your light shine before men, that they may see your good deeds and praise your Father in heaven."

John 8:2 – When Jesus spoke again to the people, He said, "I am the light of the world. Whoever follows Me will never walk in darkness, but will have the light of life."

Who Really Triumphs?

When injustice seems to triumph, Lord,
When evil seems to conquer what is right,
Sometimes, Lord, You're doing Your greatest work
When darkness seems to consume the light.
When it seems the devil is winning, Lord,
Because the world is believing his lies,
Your ultimate plan is still in motion,
And the world is in for a big surprise!

Psalm 31:24 – Be strong and take heart, all you who hope in the Lord.

1 Corinthians 1:27-29 – But God chose the foolish things of the world to shame the wise; God chose the weak things of the world to shame the strong. He chose the lowly things of this world and the despised things—and the things that are not—to nullify the things that are, so that no one may boast before Him.

Just As God Said

Have you sensed the stirrings?
Heard the rumblings from on high?
Of God's advancing legions,
Like horses in the sky?
Are you aware of a reckoning?
Of the preparations under way?
That God's plan in every detail
Is unmistakably in play?
Have you noticed how needlessly
Man struggles against what's true?
While shock waves hit the planet
Still many clearly have no clue.

Just as God said, it's happening.
Just as God said, it's clear.
Just as God said, in detail.
Just as God said, the time is near.

Luke 21:36 – "Be always on the watch and pray that you may be able to escape all that is about to happen, and that you may be able to stand before the Son of Man."

Mark 8:36 – "What good is it for a man to gain the whole world, yet forfeit his soul?"

Read: Matthew 24

The Dance

Everything is in motion
Like all the steps in a dance
Orchestrated by God,
Choreographed in advance.
Approaching the final curtain,
The last act is now on stage;
Each dancer is doing their part
As God begins to turn...
The final page.

Mark 13:26 – "At that time men will see the Son of Man coming in clouds with great power and glory. And He will send His angels and gather His elect from the four winds, from the ends of the earth to the ends of the heavens.

Mark 13:23 – "So be on your guard; I have told you everything ahead of time."

Read: Mark 13 (Signs of the End of the Age)

Revelation 22:7 – "Behold, I am coming soon! Blessed is he who keeps the words of the prophecy in this book."

"Yes, I Am"

Who was that young girl
Who said, "Yes, I am,"
When asked, "Are you a Christian?"
Then all she heard was "BLAM!!!"

At that very instant,
She stood at heaven's throne,
Lifted up by the hand of God,
As He carried her home.

Who was that young girl
Who stands taller than us all,
By admitting her faith,
One voice so loud, yet small?

With the courage of Jesus Himself,
And knowing she would die,
That very brave young girl
Has convicted you and I.

Written in 1999 after the shootings at Columbine High, where Cassie Bernall was killed. She was seventeen.

Reservations Ahead

Oh, beleaguered flock of God,
Living as aliens here,
Living for Christ in a fallen world
Makes it hard to persevere.
Though we may feel outnumbered
And be grieved by what we see,
We are kept by the power of God,
Our future secure in eternity.
So live today with joy and hope
And with the courage God gives you.
There's a place reserved in heaven
Your salvation will take you to.

1 Peter 1:8-9 – Though you have not seen Him, you love Him; and even though you do not see Him now, you believe in Him and are filled with an inexpressible and glorious joy, for you are receiving the goal of your faith, the salvation of your souls.

John 6:37 – "Whoever comes to Me I will never drive away—I shall lose none of all that He has given me, but raise them up at the last day."

John 10:28 – "I give them eternal life, and they shall never perish; no one can snatch them out of My hand."

Romans 11:29 – For God's gifts and His call are irrevocable.

In Case of Rapture

To my family and friends whom I love so dear,
In case you did not leave with me from here,
Perhaps when you find that I am gone,
Then what I said about Jesus wasn't wrong.
You'll see that others have left here, too,
And what we all told you was really true:
Jesus did come again to take us home,
And our purpose here was to make Him known.

I so often prayed that you would see
The same truth and hope of eternity,
And the love of the Father while you were here,
To know what it meant to have Him near.
The most loving things that I did say
Only seemed to push you farther away.
My flaws and weaknesses were all you could see,
Instead of God's truth living in me.

Imperfect and unworthy as I have been,
I've shown you God's truth through paintbrush and pen.
I tried my best to stay out of God's way
So you could see Him clearly on display.
But though I am gone, the truth lives on
Here in my Bible and in every new dawn.
It's not too late for you to change your mind,
But it's going to be harder on those left behind.

My prayers are still good, though I'm not here,
That you will be saved and can persevere.
Read Matthew 24, and you'll see what I mean;
God warned us ahead, and He set the scene.
He gave us His Son, the Truth and the Way,
And the Bible is God still speaking today.
It's His love letter to His children here,
Revealing through Jesus His message so clear.

Hebrews 9:28b (NKJV) – To those who eagerly wait for Him He will appear a second time, apart from sin, for salvation.

Read: Hebrews 9:24-28 and Matthew 24

I Swear

Don't you know?
Don't you know how much I love you?
Look upon that empty cross
At what my love cost.
I forgave you there.
All your sins I bear—
I swear.
If you could just believe,
You would receive
Eternal life.
What I say is true—
I promise you.

Love, Jesus

Psalm 119:160 – All your words are true; all your righteous laws are eternal.

Ephesians 3:14-19 – For this reason I kneel before the Father, from whom His whole family in heaven and on earth derives its name. I pray that out of His glorious riches He may strengthen you with power through His Spirit in your inner being, so that Christ may dwell in your hearts through faith. And I pray that you, being rooted and established in love, may have power, together with all the saints, to grasp how wide and long and high and deep is the love of Christ, and to know this love that surpasses knowledge—that you may be filled to the measure of all the fullness of God.

John 16:28 – "I came from the Father and entered the world; now I am leaving the world and going back to the Father."

John 10:9a – "I am the gate; whoever enters through me will be saved."

"I Am"

Some say I'm Jesus Christ
The Son of Man.
To some I'm just a prophet.
Who do you say I am?

Some say I'm the Son of God,
That in Him I began.
Some say I'm just a myth.
Who do you say I am?

Mark 14:61 – Again the high priest asked Him, "Are You the Christ, the Son of the Blessed One?" And Jesus said, "I am."

John 4:44 – Now we have heard for ourselves, and we know that this man really is the Savior of the world.

John 1:34 – I have seen and I testify that this is the Son of God.

Luke 9:35 – A voice came from the cloud saying, "This is my Son, whom I have chosen; listen to Him."

John 11:25 – Jesus said to her, "I am the Resurrection and the Life. He who believes in Me will live, even though he dies; and whoever lives and believes in Me will never die. Do you believe this?"

Eagle on the Wind

The young eaglet looks longingly
For hours at a time,
Into the open vastness
From her nest within the pine.
She doesn't know her place yet
Upon the silent winds;
She only knows the safety
Of her home among the limbs.

Time passes as she tests each breeze
Beneath her outstretched wings,
For she must learn to trust the wind
To bear her through all things.
Her growing faith must be complete
In what she cannot see;
It's what she feels uplifting her
She knows will set her free.

One day the sky is breathing hard;
Is it calling her to leap?
As the eagle's heart beats restlessly,
She dives into the deep.
Her heart stops for an instant
As she falls into the sky,
But as her wings reach outward,
She is caught and lifted high.

Soaring peacefully upon the wind,
Her life has been set free—
Her heart rejoices in a song
As she calls to you and me.

Hebrews 11:1 – Now faith is being sure of what we hope for and certain of what we do not see.

Prayer of Salvation

If you have never accepted Jesus Christ as your Lord
and Savior, and would like to, all you have to do is
pray a simple prayer something like this, and truly believe
what you are praying in your heart:

"Heavenly Father, I need You. I know I am a sinner, living my life
separated from You. Please forgive me. I believe You sacrificed
Your Son, Jesus, who willingly died on the cross and rose again for
me, and I thank You now for that. I accept Jesus as my Lord and Savior.
Right this moment I give You my heart and life. I turn myself
over to You. Cleanse me of all my sins. Make me the person You
created me to be.

In Your Son's precious name I pray, Amen."

1 John 4:15 – If anyone acknowledges that Jesus is the Son of God, God lives in him and he in God.

Romans 10:8-13 – …The word is near you; it is in your mouth and in your heart, that is, the word of faith we are proclaiming; that if you confess with your mouth, "Jesus is Lord," and believe in your heart that God raised Him from the dead, you will be saved. For it is with your mouth that you confess and are saved. As the Scripture says, "Anyone who trusts in Him will never be put to shame." For there is no difference between Jew and Gentile—the same Lord is Lord of all who call on Him, for, "Everyone who calls on the name of the Lord will be saved."

Welcome to the family of God! Now, you need to tell someone and find a Bible teaching church (not a religion) and fellowship with other born-again Christians who can encourage you in your new-found faith in Jesus Christ. You may discover now, that the Bible makes sense to you, though it didn't before, because it is God's love letter to His children, and now that you are His new, adopted child and He is your Father, His love letter to you will have meaning like it never did before.

See you in heaven!

CPSIA information can be obtained
at www.ICGtesting.com
Printed in the USA
FSHW012305121119
64033FS